LEADING THE LEAR

Education management books for schools from Lemos & Crane
Series Editors: Gaynor Smith and Hugh Figgess

Other related titles in this series:

Governing Schools Through Policy
Jackie Walters and Colin Richardson

Collaborative School Self-Review
Sheila Russell

For more information:

Lemos & Crane
20 Pond Square
Highgate
London N6 6BA

Tel: 0181-348 8363
Fax: 0181-347 5740
Email: admin@lemos.demon.co.uk

Leading the Learning School

Kath Aspinwall

Lemos&**Crane**

This edition first published in Great Britain 1998
Lemos & Crane
20 Pond Square
Highgate
London N6 6BA

© Kath Aspinwall 1998

ISBN 1-898001-56-1

A CIP catalogue record for this book is available from the British Library.

Design and formatting by DAP Ltd, London
Printed and bound by Redwood Books, Trowbridge.

Contents

Introduction 1

Chapter 1: What is a Learning Organisation 3

Chapter 2: How Do We Learn? 27

Chapter 3: Organisational Learning 51

Chapter 4: Schools as Learning Organisations 71

Chapter 5: What Gets in the Way of Learning? 95

Chapter 6: Leadership in the Learning School 119

Sources 151

Index 155

List of Activities

1.1 Using Metaphorical Thinking 8

1.2 Mental Models 12

1.3 Assessing the School's Stage of Consciousness 15

1.4 How Well Does Your School Encourage Learning 19

2.1 Pupil and Teacher Learning 28

2.2 Reflecting on Learning 31

2.3 Valuing Difference 37

2.4 Managing Blocks to Learning 39

2.5 Team Roles 43

2.6 I, We, They 48

3.1 The View From Here 52

3.2 Balancing and Developing the School's Organisational
Learning Styles 69

4.1 Stakeholder Analysis 74

4.2 What Is This Learning For? The How/Why Ladder 76

4.3 The 11 Characteristics of the Learning Company
Questionnaire 81

4.4 The Energy Flow Activity 90

4.5 Defining Your Learning School 93

5.1 The Organisational Toxicity Index (OTI) 96

5.2 Demands, Choices and Constraints 105

5.3 The Problem of Commitment 112

5.4 Working With The Shadow 117

6.1 Defining Leadership 122

6.2 Theories of Leadership 127

6.3 Manifesting Leadership 131

6.4 Your Power Inventory 137

6.5 Leadership and Organisational Learning 147

Introduction

Teachers and educationalists have been going through a period of turbulence, beset by criticism from without and self doubt from within. There is a need to draw upon all the resources that are available, and schools are increasingly looking to the world outside education for models, systems and structures that will help them to respond more effectively to constant pressure and demands for change.

This book concentrates on the learning that is essential to survive in turbulent times. It is designed to offer insight, ideas and activities to help teachers to identify the kind of learning that is needed and the factors that will enhance it. The book focuses on the concept of the *learning organisation*, in particular, as a creative framework for thinking. This is partly because this approach encourages teachers to regain their sense of control, to feel that they are agents rather than victims, to have confidence in their professional skills and to take responsibility for their own learning and leadership. However, it goes beyond the individual to the learning that is necessary within teams, across the whole school and within its community if real progress is to be made. In the context of becoming a learning organisation, the writing reifies the school into some kind of a being that in itself can learn. This is not simply to be read as shorthand for 'all those working within a school'. It is a recognition that an organisation is more than a sum of its parts; that the combination of staff and pupils within a school, its history and present purpose, its place in its community and many other factors give it a particular and developing identity which can usefully be comprehended as a living being.

The book is intended to be accessible and practical without over-simplifying the core ideas. It combines informative text, models and ideas, activities designed for personal or group work and glimpses or examples of the ideas in action. It is written for all those with an interest in thinking at the level of the whole school and how it works as well as about themselves and the teams to which they belong. It is also concerned with the issue of leadership at all levels in schools and the part this can play in enhancing organisational learning. It will, therefore, be relevant to all those who are playing, or would like to play, a part in providing leadership in education.

This is not a route offering formulaic, standardised, externally assessed procedures to work through. Nor is it easy. Developing the characteristics of a learning school will require time and effort but there are potentially great rewards for teachers, pupils and the whole school community.

CHAPTER 1

What Is a Learning Organisation?

The term learning organisation is relatively new. It is both immediately attractive - who could be against such a notion - and difficult to understand - how can an *organisation* learn? If schools are places of learning (and this is a big question in itself) does this mean that they are therefore automatically learning organisations? Fullan is unequivocal that they are not:

> "The school is not now a learning organization.
> Irregular waves of change, episodic projects,
> fragmentation of effort, and grinding overload is the
> lot of most schools." (Fullan, 1993: p 42)

As a consequence, teachers are tired and often demoralised. Imposed change takes it out of you! It is only possible to thrive on change when you are able to learn fast enough to keep up, and where there is a feeling of at least being in some control. To make matters worse even the most rapid and effective learning at the individual level is unlikely to be enough to manage the constant changes. Something more is needed at the level of the whole school. As Revans suggests:

> "For an organisation to survive, its rate of learning
> must be equal to or greater than the rate of change in
> its external environment." (Garratt 1987: p26)

The recent climate of apportioning blame and imposing solutions has had considerable cost. It is hard to imagine that teachers who feel de-skilled, de-professionalised and devalued can be the best promoters of learning in children and young people. Teachers must, of course, reflect critically on what they do, respond to society's anxieties, learn new skills, adapt and change their practice. Such activity is most likely to succeed within an atmosphere of purpose and hope. There is always a danger in education that schools become more concerned with sorting and labelling pupils in order to identify those who would benefit most from the next stage of education than they are about enhancing the potential of all - pupils and staff. The emphasis in the last few years has been on keeping going and getting through. But teachers and heads need something greater to aspire to, a sense that they can make a worthwhile difference. They need a bigger purpose for their overall learning and development than just surviving. I hope that the aspiration to become a learning organisation, along with some explanation of how a school might move to become one, will provide a way forward.

It is a matter for serious thought that the proponents of organisational learning have not rushed to schools as a sure and certain reservoir of good practice in this area. If schools are not truly committed to learning in the widest sense, there must be something seriously wrong. If this is the case then what must be done?

What is a learning organisation?

Organisational learning is a relatively new concept. However, some people have been working with this idea since the late 1960s and interest has expanded rapidly from the late 1980s. The terms "learning organisation" and "learning company" can be traced back to the notion of a "learning system" discussed by Revans in 1969 and Schon in his Reith Lectures of 1970: "Beyond the Stable State".

Argyris and Schon wrote about organisational learning in the late 1970s. They recognised that no amount of individual development will alone produce an organisation able to change itself as a whole.

> "... it is clear that organizational learning is not the same thing as individual learning, even when the individuals who learn are members of the organization. There are too many cases in which organizations know less than their members. There are even cases in which the organization cannot seem to learn what every member knows." (Argyris and Schon, 1978: p9)

All of us recognise this situation. On one INSET course, when headteachers were asked to draw their "image of headship", alongside the plate spinners and jugglers, it was not uncommon to find pictures of heads on the decks of large oil tankers. These were often surging onwards, unable to stop or turn in time to avoid the great rocks of change strewn in their paths despite the waves and cries of those on board.

Is it a fad?

It is possible to see the concept of the learning organisation as one of the latest in a long line of management "solutions" or fads following in the footsteps of the 1980s' "search for excellence" initiated by Peters and Waterman (1982). Within five years many of their excellent organisations had already lost their place in that particular league table (see, for example, Pascale 1990). Quite quickly, and in a way that cannot have been anticipated by these authors, it became clear that achieving excellence at one time is not enough to guarantee it in perpetuity.

There are intrinsic reasons for being attracted to the concept of becoming a learning school. Even in these more competitive and utilitarian times, most teachers are likely to be drawn to an idealistic or philosophical commitment to a notion of learning. Fullan constantly reminds us that "education has a moral purpose .... to make a difference to the lives of students regardless of background". (Fullan 1993: p4). He quotes Sarason (1990: p163):

> "Should not our aim be to judge whatever we do for our children in our schools by the criterion of how we

are fostering the desire to continue to learn about self, others, and the world, to live in the world of ideas and possibilities, to see the life span as an endless, intellectual and personal quest for knowledge and meaning." (Fullan, 1993: p45).

Is it a metaphor?

The term learning organisation is also a metaphor. It implies something unfinished - a process of learning rather than an item learned. Think for a moment what image the term learning organisation summons up in your head? Take your thinking about your school into the metaphorical by moving away from words for a moment and representing it as a picture. What does it look like? Are there lots of gaps and boundaries between the individuals and parts within it? Is it full of movement and energy? Who is at the centre and who at the periphery? What are the forces surrounding it?

This kind of thinking can be particularly useful for a group of people who want to explore their perceptions of their school and how it works. Once people are convinced that being asked to draw their organisation is not a test of their artistic skill, this can be an entertaining and insightful exercise. Examples include drawing a college as a smart briefcase and a department as a cheap supermarket carrier bag. In response to the question, "If your school were a means of transport what would it be?" a teacher drew her school as a double decker bus with no driver and no destination. Getting outside our normal frameworks for thinking can provide important illumination on how our organisation works and what might need to be changed.

Morgan explores the power of metaphors in great depth in his book *Images of Organization* (1997). He identifies eight possible metaphors, describing organisations as:

- Machines: made up of interlocking parts, each playing a clearly defined role in the functioning of the whole.

- Organisms: living rather than mechanical beings that are born, develop and die, are suited to their environments and adapt to changing circumstances.

- Brains: able to process information, develop frames of reference and learn.

- Cultures: with values, ideas, beliefs, norms and rituals.

- Political systems: with different sets of interests, power struggles, conflicts, winners and losers.

- Psychic prisons: where people are trapped within their own view of the world, their own thoughts, views and beliefs, unable to see alternatives.

- Flux and transformation: where there are four possibilities, self producing systems, chaos and complexity, circular flows of positive and negative feedback, and where every phenomenon generates its opposite in perpetual motion.

- Instruments of domination: using their employees, their host economy and the world economy to achieve their own ends. (Morgan, 1997: pp6-7).

If you are not used to thinking in this way, these may at first sight seem fanciful. A primary teacher given this list on a programme was initially puzzled, "I think I can see my school as a culture or perhaps an organism but I can't really relate to any of the others". A fellow course participant intervened:

> "What about a political system. Surely individuals in your school try to impress or influence the head or form alliances with each other. Also, in my experience, many infant schools are very comfortable psychic prisons where it is very difficult to question the orthodoxy."

In his book Morgan explores the strengths and limitations of understanding our organisation in these different ways. Our perceptions of what is going on in particular situations or what it is possible for us to do will be very different if we think of our school as a political system, for example, than it will if we think of it as a machine. Our perception of the kind of organisation we are in will almost certainly influence our behaviour for better or worse, for, as Morgan points out, however illuminating we may find our perception it is always also "a way of not seeing". He places the learning organisation within the chapter on "Organisations as Brains" but there are also links with the notion of organisations as organisms and cultures. You can consider the power of metaphorical thinking for yourself in Activity 1.1.

Activity 1.1   Using Metaphorical Thinking

Draw a picture that represents the way in which you see your school.

Can you see elements of the following metaphors in your picture:
Machines (e.g. interlocking parts)
Organisms (e.g. signs of growth or decay)
Brains (e.g. connections or learning)
Cultures (e.g. signs or symbols)
Political systems (e.g. significant groupings)
Psychic prisons (e.g. strong boundaries)

Flux and transformation (e.g. movement and energy)
Instruments of domination (e.g. dominant and submissive figures)

Which seem most applicable to your school and why?

```
┌──────────────────────────────────────────────────────┐
│                                                        │
│                                                        │
│                                                        │
│                                                        │
│                                                        │
│                                                        │
└──────────────────────────────────────────────────────┘
```

Have you any further metaphors of your own to add?

```
┌──────────────────────────────────────────────────────┐
│                                                        │
│                                                        │
│                                                        │
│                                                        │
│                                                        │
│                                                        │
└──────────────────────────────────────────────────────┘
```

What insight have you gained by thinking about your school in this way?

```
┌──────────────────────────────────────────────────────┐
│                                                        │
│                                                        │
│                                                        │
│                                                        │
│                                                        │
│                                                        │
└──────────────────────────────────────────────────────┘
```

(Based on Morgan, 1977)

9

How can we understand the concept?

In attempting to explain the concept or the principle of the learning organisation, writers provide a variety of models, disciplines and characteristics. Senge describes:

> "...organizations where people continually expand their capacity to create the results they truly desire, where new and expansive patterns of thinking are nurtured, where collective aspiration is set free, and where people are continually learning how to learn together." (Senge, 1990: p.3)

He proposes that there are crucial disciplines to be mastered (1990: pp 6-16).

Five disciplines for the learning organisation

These are as follows:

- Personal mastery

- Sharing mental models

- Building shared vision

- Team learning

- Systems thinking.

1. Personal mastery

This discipline is centred on individual self-development. Senge stresses the importance of "continually clarifying and deepening our personal vision, of focusing our energies, of developing patience and of seeing reality objectively". This is a life-long process through which we seek to deepen our purposes and engage in continuous learning so that we can become able to fulfil our potential.

On the whole, teachers who have lost their sense of personal vision are not happy people and will find it difficult to contribute to a learning school. On an in-service training day for teachers, two individuals from the same school manifested quite different behaviours. One was actively engaged in everything that went on, the other slumped in his chair. At one point the participants were asked why they taught. What were their aspirations? The first teacher sat forward in his chair. "This is probably going to sound silly," he said, "but still I love teaching. I really want to give pupils an understanding of history. I want to get them interested and excited so that they want to know more..." When it came to the second teacher, he hardly stirred. "I used to feel like that," he said, "but it's hopeless. They don't care about French, the parents don't support you and I'm only in it for the brown envelope at the end of the month. It's absolutely hopeless." He was only too clearly not a happy man.

2. Sharing mental models

We all have preconceptions and assumptions: our worldview or mental models. These influence both what we see and what we do. Many disagreements occur because we not understand each other's perceptions of a problem. Conversely, our shared assumptions can become so powerful that they cannot be challenged. Some mental models are personal but many are shared by groups or more widely. The history of education can be interpreted as a series of beliefs, models, certainties about the purpose and practice of schooling, following one from another, occurring and recurring, growing, dominating then declining.

One is often most conscious of a dominant mental model when it is not shared, when one is out of step or out of fashion. Some schools' whole identity seems to be bound up in their particular view of the world of education. Others are more pragmatic. Different countries also take different stances. For example, children start their formal education earlier in the UK than almost anywhere else in the world. Until recently this was almost never questioned. It is seldom discussed as an issue when concern is expressed about Britain's place in world attainment tables. Most parents still believe that the sooner their child goes to school the better his or her future chances. This may or may not be true but the interesting issue is that it is often not open to discussion. Our shared mental model is too powerful for this to happen. Reflect on what is discussable in your school by considering the questions in Activity 1.2.

Activity 1.2   **Mental Models**

Make a list of all the educational issues that you recollect having been talked about in staff meetings or the staff room recently.

Are you conscious of things that do not seem to be discussable?

What happens when someone tries to raise such issues?

What are pupils allowed or not allowed to discuss?

What are the implications of the dominant mental models in your school?

(Based on Senge, 1990)

It is not always reaction from others that prevents us from speaking. Sometimes we stay quiet because of self-censorship - because we do not want to rock the boat. If we value our relationship with a colleague or we recognise that, come what may, we have to rub along together we may choose not to raise issues that might lead us to disagree. To think as a collective in the learning organisation, we need to encourage dialogue as well as debate so that the diversity of personal and shared constructs of the world are explored. Senge (1990: pp201-2) proposes a process for opening up and challenging mental models:

- Make your own reasoning explicit - say how you came to this view

- Encourage others to explore your view

- Encourage others to provide different views

- Actively inquire into others' views

- If you reach an impasse ask if there is any way in which you could both/all carry out some further enquiry

- Try to be open in thinking about what might be causing the problem between you.

Becoming better at sharing mental models helps with the building of the next discipline.

3. Shared vision
This involves those working in a school working together to build a shared picture of the future that fosters "genuine commitment and enrolment rather than compliance". This can lead people to "excel and learn, not because they are told to but because they want to". We will be returning to the issue of vision in more detail in Chapter 6.

4. Team learning
Most of us have had the experience of working in a team which

really gels, and where we worked so well together that it becomes hard in retrospect to know who thought of what. Such teams form key units in the learning organisation. The discipline of team learning involves dialogue - the capacity to creatively explore ideas and suspend our own judgements in a free-flow of meaning whereby the team "thinks" as a single organism. This discipline is explored in much more detail in Chapter 2.

5. Systems thinking

The "fifth discipline" underpins and integrates all the others. This discipline requires "destroying the illusion that the world is created of separate, unrelated forces" and, says Senge (1990: p.73), enables us to see "interrelationships rather than linear cause effect chains", and also to see "processes of change rather than snapshots".

This capacity is of fundamental importance. Systems thinking is a methodology for seeing in wholes and for recognising the patterns and the inter-relatedness of parts which go to make up these wholes. This discipline requires us to work with the patterns, relationships and subtle interconnections of the learning organisation as a living system. At the micro level, Senge proposes that systems thinking leads to the development of understanding and purpose; we no longer feel helpless in the face of "the system". At a macro level systems thinking is essential for our survival: "We are literally killing ourselves because of our inability to understand wholes." (Senge, 1991: p42.)

An organisation's consciousness

A further perspective is provided by Pedler, Burgoyne and Boydell, who describe the learning organisation as:

> "an organisation that facilitates the learning of all its members *and* consciously transforms itself and its context" (Pedler, Burgoyne and Boydell, 1997: p1).

They stress that busyness and taking prompt action to respond to whatever is happening to or around an organisation is not enough. The purpose of action is, firstly, to resolve the immediate problem but secondly, and importantly, to learn from that process. They see organisations as evolving through three stages of consciousness. The first of these is **surviving** and requires the development of habits and processes that enable organisations to carry out their basic task and deal with problems as they arise. A school at this stage of development may be responsive but is constantly surprised by the changes it is asked to make. It may react to each change as it comes along but without having any overall clarity of purpose within which to set the change into context.

At the **adapting** stage organisations become competent at reading their environment and making any changes necessary to adapt to what will be needed. In such schools there will be a constant effort to keep up to date with political and educational trends. For example, adjusting to the requirements of the *Framework for Inspection* long before the letter announcing the date for the school to be inspected arrives.

At the third **sustaining** stage, organisations achieve a relationship with their environments where they can create, as well as respond to, their context. Schools at this stage will be building links with parents, employers and the local TEC, contributing to the school's page of the local paper, working on research and development projects with at least one university. (Pedler *et al*, 1997: pp4-5)

Now measure your school against the stages set out in Activity 1.3.

Activity 1.3   **Assessing the school's stage of consciousness**

Surviving   Adapting   Sustaining

☐☐☐☐☐☐☐☐☐☐

Where would you place your school?

What evidence do you have to support your claim?

What are you learning from your experiences?

What else might you do?

Creating a learning school

While schools may not yet be learning organisations it is clear that some schools learn faster and better than others. For example, Rosenholtz found that it is "far easier to learn to teach and to learn to teach better, in some schools than in others"(Rosenholtz, 1989: p104). Fullan is a particularly rich source of information, ideas and models of the ways in which schools are developing their capacity to learn. In *Change Forces* (1993), and in earlier books written with Hargreaves, he draws together examples from a number of educational writers and researchers (Little, Rosenholtz, Nias, Southworth, Yoemans, Louis and Miles and many others) who all, in one form or another, stress the importance of creating collaborative, integrative, developmental and learning cultures. Such schools see themselves as part of a neighbourhood, a wider community, a region, a nation and ultimately the world. This is important as:

> "The societies that appear to be adapting most successfully are those that have historically placed a very high value on learning, and regard it as a lifelong process." (CIAR, 1992: p22)

In explaining her finding that learning occurs more easily in some schools than others, Rosenholtz (1989) identifies two categories of school:

1. 'Stuck' or 'learning impoverished' schools characterised by

- teacher isolation/privatism
- lack of positive feedback
- uncertainty
- avoidance of risk taking
- a sense of powerlessness.

2. 'Moving' or 'learning enriched' schools characterised by

- collaboration and sharing
- continuous teacher talk about practice
- a common focus
- a sense of efficacy

- a belief in life-long learning
- looking out as well as in.

The contrast between being 'stuck' and 'moving' is a powerful one, although schools that are stuck are not necessarily unhappy. Staff working in isolation may present few challenges to each other, colluding in an unspoken agreement not to rock the boat. However, isolation and fragmentation dissipate energy. Practical action is indicated. Teachers must talk to each other, plan together, and identify a sense of common purpose. The energy to move must be created.

Some years ago a head teacher took over a primary school after it had been run by an autocratic head for many years. The staff in the school were truly stuck. They preferred it that way. The head was able to appoint two new staff but they had little immediate impact against the prevailing culture. She was, however, an enthusiastic learner herself and was taking an Open University diploma, which focused on the teaching of reading. She would frequently go into the staffroom at breaks to discuss what she was learning: "Do you know, I have been teaching reading for years and yet I had not realised... Have any of you noticed this? Look out for it and please let me know."

For the first time people began to find it possible to acknowledge their own learning. It became 'normal' to discuss what was going on behind those closed classroom doors. They were encouraged to go on courses. The new staff were the first to take up this opportunity but the idea began to catch on. The school began, slowly at first but with increasing energy, to move.

Benefits of a learning enriched school

Individual teachers who are strongly committed to their own learning and development are unlikely to feel totally dependent on courses provided by others. They will be likely to have more than one learning style (see Chapter 2). They will build in some systematic reflection and ongoing evaluation into their practice. They will find fellow learners - in their own school if there is a general aspiration to be a learning organisation, and somewhere else if not. They will look for challenge as well as support from others. They will talk with others about what they do and why they do it, and perhaps create new knowledge together. When they go on courses, they will have high expectations of content and process alongside a real commitment to participation and learning. They will not expect to be spoon-fed and entertained. They will read books, journal articles, keep up to date with the news, and will not be constantly surprised and unready for the next set of changes. They will be ready to learn new skills to meet new situations but will have their own purposes and their own developmental path.

This commitment and energy can be greatly enhanced when the learning extends beyond the individual. Teachers aspiring to create a learning school will not only take a positive approach to their own learning but will also place considerable emphasis on learning with and through colleagues. There are many such teachers in our schools and many more with this potential who have somehow lost their energy or their way. All are likely to be affected, for good or ill, by the wider climate in the schools within which they teach. Learning together and colleagueship are often emphasised in the writing on learning schools and organisations. Nias et al (1989) found that in highly collaborative schools "the individual and the group are simultaneously valued".

At this stage make an initial diagnosis of the school in which you work. The questionnaire in Activity 1.4 helps you to consider how conducive your school is to learning.

Activity 1.4	How well does your school encourage learning?

Are there many ways of learning or just a few? Many ☐ Few ☐

Do you talk about staff learning as well as pupils' learning? Yes ☐ No ☐

Is knowledge and expertise valued?

Yes ☐ No ☐

Is learning valued?

Yes ☐ No ☐

Is there an expectation that people will learn from each other?

Yes ☐ No ☐

Are all people - whatever their job - expected to learn?

Yes ☐ No ☐

Is there evidence that the head and SMT are learning and changing?

Yes ☐ No ☐

Does action usually lead to learning?

Yes ☐ No ☐

Does learning often lead to a change in what is done?

Yes ☐ No ☐

Do people take time out for reflection?

Yes ☐ No ☐

Does the school learn from other organisations?

Yes ☐ No ☐

Is the school well connected to its community?

Yes ☐ No ☐

How well does your school do?

What could you do to improve or transform the situation?

How much do you know about:
• how people learn in your school?

• how people learn in other schools?

• how your school can do better?

What kind of learning is needed?

Learning is a word much used in schools (as well as in this chapter) but its meaning is less often debated. One way of understanding learning is to break it into four different types (Pedler and Aspinwall, 1996: p.25):

1. Knowledge, i.e. learning *about* things

2. Skills, Abilities, Competencies, i.e. learning to *do* things

3. Personal development, i.e. learning to *become ourselves, to achieve our full potential*

4. Collaborative enquiry, i.e. learning to *achieve things together.*

The first two of these types of learning - knowledge, and skills, abilities, competencies - are the most familiar. Learning *about* things covers a wide spectrum, from the memorising of simple facts to the deep understanding of complex ideas, and ranges from knowing "this or that" to knowing "why". Learning to *do* things includes mental and manual skills and competence in certain situations. These two concepts of learning have great significance for schools. The development of the National Curriculum in the UK was an attempt to define what type of knowledge should form the basis of schooling and thus has been a matter of some dispute since its inception. These two types of learning are seen as relatively discrete by some who place importance on maintaining an academic/vocational divide.

The introduction of NVQs and GNVQs has led to endless debate about the place and value of these different kinds of learning. The gulf between the two and the difference in status seems to be greater in the UK than almost anywhere else in the world. Pring argues strongly against this dualism:

"If we respect both the learner and those cultural resources upon which that learning must draw - then there seems to be no reason why the liberal should

not be conceived as something vocationally useful
and why the vocationally useful should not be taught
in an educational and liberating way." (Pring, 1995:
p 183)

Pring advocates focusing on what it means to be a whole person as the basis for bridging this divide. This, the third type of learning, is about achieving our full potential. It goes beyond intellectual and competency development to questions of purpose and identity, echoed in Murdoch's "learning is moral progress" (1992). Personal development has long been valued in schools and in adult education, although it has been seriously threatened in recent years by the increasingly utilitarian approach to education. Adult education funding has been directed towards courses linked to qualifications or employment rather than valuing a broader definition of human development. The school curriculum has become crowded. Courses for teachers have increasingly emphasised gaining the knowledge and skills relevant to the imposed changes. Schools are learning how to conform to an imposed framework of inspection. Knowledge, skills and competence, and meeting inspection requirements are clearly necessary to teachers but are not enough in themselves. To quote the head teacher from a primary school who had found the inspection of her school to be a useful, developmental and stabilising experience:

"I have only one reservation. If the framework
becomes dominant in our thinking, and if the
inspectors spend all their time inspecting, where will
the new ideas and creativity and the 'magic' come
from in the future?"

The fourth type of learning is less often recognised. Learning is most often seen as something which individuals do on their own, and happening, somehow, inside them. Collaborative enquiry is more than effective group work. It is about learning to achieve things together, co-operating in collective learning, creating new ideas and possibilities, seeing familiar things in unfamiliar ways. There is an interesting historical precedent. Samuel Hartlib (1600-1662) and his associates proposed an early sort of learning community when they created the "Office of Addresses" for the spreading of scientific knowledge during the ferment of the Commonwealth parliament. They often published anonymously or collaboratively under one name because their work was "all in a knot of one another's labours".

Collaborative enquiry, where outcomes cannot be fully measured in terms of what individuals take away but by what is created together, is a powerful source of learning. However, it is not always fully valued. Teachers are under pressure to measure individual learning in pupils. In all sorts of organisations individual appraisal systems also suggest that individual development is what matters. However, recognising and placing a higher value on learning that we create together can form the bridge to take us from learning within individuals towards the learning organisation.

Four key characteristics of the learning school

There is much still to be said about the nature of the learning school but it is possible even at this stage to pull out of this chapter the essence and fundamental characteristics that are necessary to achieve this ideal. A learning school is an organisation where there is:

- A commitment to lifelong learning for *all* those within the school

- An emphasis on collaborative learning and the creative and positive use of difference and conflict

- An holistic understanding of the school as an organisation

- Strong connections and relationships with the community and the world outside the school.

None of these, or the various skills, attitudes, relationships touched on in this chapter, are revolutionary or unfamiliar to teachers. Many groups of staff work to attain them, many prospective head teachers speak of their intention to foster just such cultures. All of these characteristics will be explored and developed in the rest of this book.

The issue of how we learn as individuals and in teams and groups will be explored in some detail in the Chapter 2. The more difficult issue, that of how to develop a holistic understanding of the whole school is considered in the next two chapters. Chapter 3 provides several different ways to help you to conceive of your school as a whole and then looks at different organisational learning styles. Chapter 4 looks first at the crucial issue of purpose and what all this learning is for. It then provides two different models for thinking about your school and how it works as an organisation and an activity to help you to pull together your own ideas of what you would expect to find in a learning school. Chapter 5 looks at the various factors that may hinder learning. Chapter 6 considers the issue of leadership and in particular the kind of leadership that is needed to infuse the whole of a learning school. It might be expected that the issue of leading would be addressed at the beginning of the book. But it is only when the kind of organisation we want to create is resolved, and the kinds of relationships we want to develop within it clarified, that we can turn to the matter of what kind of leadership we will need.

CHAPTER 2

How Do
We Learn?

In *Zen and the Art of Motor Cycle Maintenance*, Peirsig describes a welder at work:

> "He sparks the torch, and sets a tiny little blue flame
> and then, it's hard to describe, actually dances the
> torch and the rod in separate little rhythms over the
> thin sheet metal, the whole spot a uniform, luminous
> orange-yellow, dropping the torch and filler rod
> down at exactly the right moment and then removing
> them. No holes. You can hardly see the weld. 'That's
> beautiful,' I say." (Peirsig, 1974: p360)

What is happening here is more than the exhibition of a practical skill. Where does this extra quality of work - the beauty - come from? How was it learned? Can this dimension be taught? Can it be tested and what might be helped or hindered were we to try? This chapter looks at the issue of how we learn as individuals and in teams and groups.

What is learning?

Learning is, or should be, a matter of great interest to teachers but one of the problems is that it can be very hard to pin down. Teachers' attention is also most often directed to the learning of others, "Have they learned what we have taught them?" The Open University study pack, *Curriculum in Action* (1980) is based on six apparently straightforward questions:

- What did the pupils actually do?

- What were they learning?

- How worthwhile was it?

- What did I do?

- What did I learn?

- What do I intend to do now?

These fundamental questions provide an excellent framework for evaluating and understanding what happens in classrooms and for focusing on teacher as well as pupil learning. Answering them fully takes considerable time and effort but they repay even relatively superficial attention. Try to answer the questions in Activity 2.1 by drawing on a recent teaching episode.

| Activity 2.1 | **Pupil and teacher learning** |

Think of a recent teaching activity or lesson:
- What did the pupils actually do?

- What were they learning?

• How worthwhile was it?

• What did I do?

• What did I learn?

• What do I intend to do now?

(Based on Open University, 1980)

How well did you do in answering these questions? As with all good questions these lead to many more. For example: Has the emphasis on assessment made you more skilled than you used to be? What might you be missing? What do you mean by 'worthwhile-ness'? Is this definition shared by your colleagues? In what ways are the learning of teachers and children or young people the same? How are they different? Do you need to ask yourself these questions again in the future, perhaps while you are teaching?

The National Curriculum and the requirement for assessment and testing has made it impossible for teachers to retreat from the problem of trying to identify and quantify pupil learning. The assessment of trainee teachers is also increasingly specific and competence based. This inevitably pushes us towards assessing that which can be more easily measured. There is growing concern that we are learning to value what we can measure rather than learning to measure what we value. An additional problem is that an overwhelming emphasis on task and performance may have the inherent problem of being antithetical to meaningful learning. Coad draws together work from a number of educational psychologists who differentiate between learning and performing to provide the following table (based on Coad, 1996):

	Learning orientation	Performance orientation
Success defined as	Mastering the task	Outperforming others
Value placed on	Developing new skills	Demonstrating skills to important others
View of learning	Learning is valued	Reluctance to experiment
View of effort	Mastery and effort directly related	Effort is given to outperforming others
Locus of interest	Intrinsic interest in work	Extrinsic interest in work
View of mistakes	Part of learning process	Elicit anxiety
Choice of task	Preference for challenge	Avoid challenge for fear of failure

This suggests that over-emphasis on performance may result in a diminution of learning. This has considerable implication for schools facing the increased demand for setting targets and business planning. Having a common purpose and something tangible to aim for can be helpful and motivating and there is no way of ignoring this pressure completely, but we must take care that we do not let this emphasis on task and outcomes result in the neglect of process and learning.

This chapter is focusing on *how* not *what* you learn. It offers some ways of understanding how *you* do this both as an individual and in groups and teams. The next activity asks you to focus on yourself and how you learn by asking you to reflect for a moment on something you learned about your work or yourself as a teacher recently.

Activity 2.2	Reflecting on learning

Think about something that you learned recently about your work or yourself as a teacher:

- What did you learn?
- How did you learn it?
- Which factors helped you to learn?
- What changed as a result/how do you know that you learned it?

Now think of something you resisted learning:

- What did you resist learning?
- Why did you resist it?
- Which factors hindered your learning?

Now summarise your conclusions on the diagram below remembering to include factors within yourself as well as those from outside.

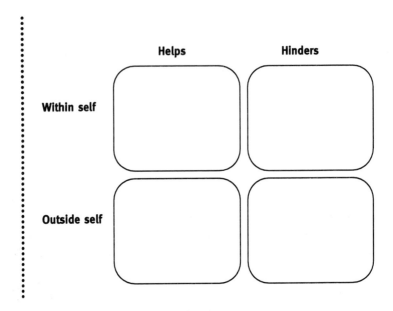

	Helps	Hinders
Within self		
Outside self		

Many different factors influence our learning. Some of these are external, such as the place in which we work or the pressure we are under. But our response to these will be influenced at least in part by our individual reactions, and by the kind of person that we are. The same external factor may influence us differently at different times or in different circumstances. For example, have you ever reread, after an interval of several years, a novel that had a great impact on you at an earlier stage in your life? It is unlikely that it felt like the same experience the second time around. In reflecting on the difference we realise how much our circumstances, our worldview, and we ourselves have changed.

George Kelly believed that learning is fundamental to life:

> "Learning is not a special class of psychological processes; it is synonymous with any and all psychological processes. It is not something that happens to a person on occasion; it is what makes him a person in the first place." (Kelly, 1955: p75)

However encouraging it may be that one is always somehow learning something, it does not feel enough to take us forward.

Why is it, for example, that we seem to learn more effectively in some circumstances than others, and why is useful learning from experience by no means guaranteed?

Learning styles

One of the most familiar ideas in the area of individual learning is David Kolb's learning cycle (see Figure 2.1). He suggests that when we are learning we move through a repeating cycle of four stages: concrete experiences, observation and reflection, formation of abstract concepts and generalisations, and testing the implications of concepts in new situations. Sometimes this is presented more simply.

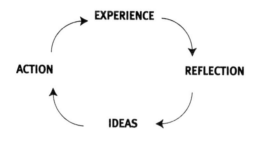

Figure 2.1 Kolb's learning cycle

We do not, however, move effortlessly and regularly through this process. Sometimes we get stuck at one or another stage or prefer to cycle between just two. Most of us feel much more comfortable in particular stages of the cycle than others: some people are more reflective; some leap into action straight away; others prefer to think and conceptualise. Kolb has developed a Learning Style Inventory which is designed to describe *how* you learn, not to measure your learning ability (Kolb, 1971). Different preferences may lead us into different areas of work and these in their turn will accentuate particular styles of learning. For example, Kolb suggests that a mathematician will tend to emphasise abstract concepts, a poet may value concrete experience, managers are often preoccupied with putting ideas into action, while a naturalist will be concerned to develop his or her skills of observation (Kolb, 1971: p28).

Any classroom will contain pupils with these contrasting preferences, only some of whom will be in tune with their teacher's preferences. An example of these differences shows up in the way that people respond to being asked to evaluate a course they have attended. After one INSET course teachers were asked to comment on the teaching styles that had been used. Fifty per cent said the mix of style had been about right, 25 per cent said it had been too didactic and 25 per cent that there had been too much activity and discussion and not enough teaching; yet they had all been together on the same course.

If you have a very strongly preferred learning style this may work very well for you in the right context but it can get in the way of learning when you are placed in a situation that requires a different approach. My experience analysing the learning style of a considerable number of teachers suggests a reasonably strong preference (probably most pronounced amongst primary teachers) for concrete experience and active experimentation; they like to do things. Any reflection and abstract conceptualisation is often somewhat cursory and this tendency has almost certainly been accentuated by the plethora of change in recent years. Busyness rules OK in many of our schools.

Much of the thinking about individual learning style has been influenced by Jung's theory of personality type (Jung 1971). Katherine Briggs and her daughter Isabel Briggs Myers have undertaken a great deal of work in developing this theory and have identified 16 different personality types based on where individual place themselves in relation to four different scales of preference (Briggs, Myers and Myers (1990).

1. *Where you prefer to focus your attention or where you turn to for energy.*
>   to/from others - Extroversion *E*
>   or
>   to/from within yourself - Introversion *I*

2. How you prefer to acquire information and make sense of the world.
>   through your five senses - Sensing *S*
>   or
>   through your imagination - Intuition *N*

3. How you prefer to make decisions.
>   impersonally/objectively - Thinking *T*
>   or
>   personally/subjectively - Feeling *F*

4. Your preferred style of behaving, how you like to organise your life.
>   planned, organised and settled - Judging *J*
>   or
>   fluid, open and flexible - Perceiving *P*

*Once you have established in which direction your preferences lie you combine the four resulting initials to name your type. For example, **ENTP, ISTJ, ESFJ.***

This is a very brief introduction to these ideas. To check out your preferences in detail and make full use of this approach you need to complete a questionnaire (see, for example, Keirsey and Bates, 1984). However, to gain a flavour of the process, you may be able to recognise yourself within one of the following brief descriptions of preferred approaches to teaching. The types have been reduced to four by combining two of the scales of preference together. These are, of course, slight caricatures but you will probably find that you can identify more with one set of characteristics than the others.

1. - a well planned classroom
  - well established routines
  - firm but fair
 	
  - active participant in
    school affairs
  - want to develop
    good citizens
	2. - an emphasis on spontaneity
	  - lots of different activities
	  - unpredictable but usually
	    benign
	  - have lots of own outside
	    interests
	  - happy to let pupils
	    develop as they will

3. - well planned lessons
   - enjoy curriculum
     development
   - set high standards

   - strongly interested
     in subject
   - value intelligence

4. - willing to abandon plans
   - involve pupils in decision
     making
   - interested in values and
     social development
   - interested in the process of
     learning
   - value relationships

If you feel that you are most like 1. you would be described as an *SJ*; 2. is an *SP*; 3. an *NT*; and 4. an *NF*.

In their studies in California, Keirsey and Bates found that the majority of teachers, 56 per cent, were SJs. NFs made up 36 per cent of the workforce, NTs 6 per cent and only 2 per cent were SPs, although this group makes up 38 per cent of the general population. SPs are generally seen to be spontaneous and pleasure seeking free spirits so perhaps it is not surprising that they are not to be found for long in the classroom. SJs, in contrast, are "impatient to be useful", filled with a desire to serve. As children they are anxious to know what they are supposed to do. Keirsey and Bates (1984: p 40) say, "School is made for SJs and largely run by SJs." NFs want to establish their personal identity but also to make a difference in the world and to humankind. Both SJs and NFs might match up to Fullan's contention, "Scratch a good teacher and you will find a moral purpose." (Fullan, 1993: p10). NTs place great value on competence and like to be able to understand, control, predict and explain reality. They are more likely to be found teaching in higher education if they are attracted to teaching at all.

Not everyone feels comfortable with the notion of personality type; some people have a strong antipathy to feeling boxed and labelled. This is not the fundamental intention. Each of the scales of preferences is a continuum; you may have a strong, moderate or weak preference. In addition this does not exclude the opposite end of the continuum entirely. A preference for making decisions on the basis of feeling, for example, does not mean that you have no capacity for thinking. Jung suggests that the purpose of the first half of life is to understand and work with your preferences while the task of the second half is to work on your neglected side.

These differences extend into the way that teachers like a school to be organised. For example, those with SJ preferences like structure and order, clear job descriptions. They are tolerant of hierarchy but not of people who do not carry out their responsibilities effectively. Those with NF inclinations tend to be more preoccupied with the climate and culture of the school. They like to work in friendly, flexible and responsive organisations and are often impatient of rules and deadlines. One of the consequences of individuals having such different preferences is that it creates difficulty in understanding each other. A person who prefers logic, order and closure will find it hard to cope with one who likes variety and wants to leave options open for as long as possible, and *vice versa*. Anyone who has ever had to teach in a team or work closely with someone with a very different style will know how hard this can be. Keirsey and Bates, Myers and Briggs take a very positive attitude to these differences in preference. They stress that the critical thing to do is to value and work with difference, complementing rather than opposing each other. Consider these questions in Activity 2.3.

Activity 2.3	**Valuing difference**

Think of a difficult recent interaction with a colleague:

What were the key differences between you?

What did you do?

How did s/he respond?

In the light of personality type theory, how might you have behaved differently, in a way that might have been more acceptable to him/her?

Are there ways in which you complement each other?

What will you do differently next time?

What gets in the way of learning

The exercise above reminds us that a problem with the notion of learning is that, although we all have a strong inclination towards it we also have well developed defences against it. Learning can be painful, confusing and often requires us to change behaviours that have become comfortable over time. As Roger Harrison explains:

"People have the conceptual systems they have
because in some important situations the systems
proved adaptive for them ... if we were to lose these
systems, we would become like ships without
rudders; we would have lost our control systems, our
chances of acting in an organised, intelligent fashion
to meet our needs." (Harrison, 1995: p187)

Any attempt by others to break down our defences against learning is almost certainly counter productive. Rather than being grateful, our first reaction is to find another, probably less adequate, defence to hide behind. Very often this is in anger and rejection of the person who threatened our protection. Anyone who has ever had to provide a learning or training event for people who were sent by somebody else, do not want to be there and do not want to know, will be aware of what a negative experience this can be for everyone.

Activity 2.4	Managing blocks to learning

What did I resist learning?

What is my preferred approach to learning?

How was this helping or hindering me in this situation?

Are there any learning possibilities that I often reject out of hand?

What might I do to extend my personal learning repertoire?

Learning in teams

The first part of this chapter has focused on individual learning. Understanding ourselves and how we learn most effectively is helpful but not enough to ensure we build a learning school. The next step is to begin to look more closely at how we work together, by focusing on learning in teams. While few people may be confident that they are working in a learning organisation, most people have experienced at some time what it is like to work in a

supportive and creative team. Senge describes team learning as one
of the five disciplines of a learning organisation and says, "If teams
learn they are a microcosm for learning throughout the
organisation." He believes that team learning has three critical
dimensions:

> "Learning to tap the potential for several minds to be
> 'more intelligent' than one; developing a capacity for
> co-ordinated action, 'operational trust'; and carrying
> this capacity into other teams." (Senge, 1990: p236).

Because what we think influences what we do, Senge also places
great emphasis on "seeing each other as colleagues":

> "Treating each other as colleagues acknowledges the
> mutual risk and establishes the sense of safety in
> facing the risk. Colleagueship does not mean that you
> need to agree or share the same view. On the
> contrary, the real power of seeing each other as
> colleagues comes into play when there are differences
> of view. It is easy to feel collegial when everyone
> agrees. When there are significant disagreements it is
> more difficult. But the pay off is much greater.
> Choosing to view 'adversaries' as 'colleagues with
> different views' has the greatest benefits." (Senge,
> 1990: p245).

It is important to recognise that a team is not the same thing as a
group. Senge uses the analogy of a sports team or a jazz band to
capture the difference. Everyone is not doing the same thing but all
are working to a common purpose. Individuals get their solo
moments but, being attuned to one another, do not dominate in a
way that distorts the overall performance.

Most schools organise themselves into teams of one kind or
another. Some are relatively stable: the senior management team,
year groups, departments, the pastoral team. Others may be
formed temporarily for a specific purpose and disband once their

task is completed. This is an important difference. Unless there is an unfortunate mix of people, there is often a good deal of energy, even excitement, in teams brought together with a specific task and time frame. This can lead to a lot of good work being done or it can result in leaping into action before things have been properly thought through.

Team building events often include the setting up of timed tasks for teams to complete. Almost always the first lesson that is learned is that rushing into action is counter productive and that the more practical or physical the tasks is, the harder it is to plan before you act. Not everyone has the chance to undertake this kind of learning safely away from their work as it is usually assumed that people know how to be good team members without any help. The often painful learning has to take place in a real situation in public, when pride may make it harder for mistakes to be owned up to and undone.

David Casey (1993) points out that it is important to be clear when real teamwork is needed. He relates this to the complexity of the task. If the task is clear and straightforward there is not a great deal of need for discussion and creative interaction; an individual or group can probably just get on with it. When things become a little more complicated there is a greater need for co-operation and planning. However, when things are complex, outcomes uncertain and there is a good deal of risk, we will need a team that can trust each other, work and engage in collaborative enquiry, and learn together to achieve the kind of synergy that is needed.

How do teams that you are part of work together? What part do you play in a team? Is it always the same part or do you change your contribution according to the context? Consider these questions by carrying out Activity 2.5. Think about a particular team and identify who performs which kind of role within it and how the team responds.

| Activity 2.5 | | | Team Roles |

Role	Who performs this role?	How are they responded to and valued?	Does performance of the role need strengthening/ weakening?
Orchestrating group resources			
Driving and shaping			
Generating lots of ideas			
Creating and maintaining harmony			
Getting the group to finish its work			
Checking progress and achievements			
Generating resources for the group			

These behaviours have been identified by Belbin (1981) as necessary if teams are to be productive. Here too you are likely to have particular strengths and preferences. However, if you are stuck in a particular way of behaving, a strength almost always becomes a weakness. This is particularly true when there is a strong bias in several people to the same kind of behaviour. For example, a group full of people concerned to maintain harmony might be very pleasant to belong to but there may not be much challenge. A group of drivers and shapers often spends more time locked in internal power struggles than in focusing on the job in hand. A framework like this can help you to reflect on how you are working together and point to the behaviours that you may need to develop more to work successfully together. How you respond to each other is a significant factor in how the team develops.

Casey (1993: p.44) takes the consideration of process as well as task a stage further and suggests that real team work demands that we pay at least as much attention to feelings as we do to getting the task done. He describes some emotion processes:

- Expressing feelings openly

- Working through conflict as it arises

- Delaying until consensus is reached

- Valuing colleagues as people

- Spending time on group development

- Acknowledging inadequacy

- Building trust

- Risking yourself as well as your thoughts

- Crying when you need to cry

- Claiming leadership of the team occasionally.

How possible would it feel to deal with all - or even some - of these issues in the teams that you belong to? What would happen were you to produce this list? Casey is describing his work with directors and chief executives in a variety of private and public organisations. He says that it may take considerable time to help a team to work with emotional processes, much longer than with task processes such as setting agendas, establishing priorities, developing review processes and so forth. However, "once both facilities are in place they work faster, more effectively and with more joy" (Casey, 1993: p 45). How much effort is your school prepared to put into helping the teams you are part of to work more effectively? Which teams might have tasks and purposes that require this level of investment? Have you ever thought of bringing in an outsider to help with this process if the team cannot manage alone?

Supporting groups and relationships

In recent years there has been much emphasis on creating productive teams that set agendas and meet deadlines and (unfortunately often) that do not ask too many questions. There are, however, other important reasons for coming together for support and learning.

Newly appointed heads are now encouraged to choose a mentor with whom to build a trusting, supportive and learning partnership. Although some heads were critical of the advisory services provided by their LEA, many miss the support of an informed school adviser who would visit regularly and to whom they could turn in times of trouble or joy.

Staff may team up for a variety of reasons particularly when there may be pain and the learning may be fruitful. A group of secondary teachers who were trying to expand their teaching repertoire found that it was helpful to try out new approaches together. In one school, teachers paired up in tutor time because they wanted to expand their repertoire of teaching skills to include the opportunity of more experiential learning. They agreed on their purposes and how they wanted to manage the experiences. Because they were in twos, they were less fearful of losing control and therefore were more relaxed and confident. They were able to point out to each other when they thought they were not behaving in the way they had planned. Without this mutual checking they were liable to slip back into 'telling' mode in the classroom. Because they had chosen to work together and were thinking of each other as peers, they were able to be open about their feelings. They became fellow learners.

An alternative, or complement, to these two-way relationships is to become part of a small group of learners, and the last kind of learning I want to consider in this context is action learning.

Action Learning

This is an approach to management education developed by Reg Revans and it provides the opportunity for people to come together to learn within the context of some useful principles and processes. Revans believes that action and learning are intimately connected: "There can be no learning without action and no (sober and deliberate) action without learning." (Revans, 1983: p54). He describes learning as having two elements: the first is traditional instruction or *programmed knowledge* and the second critical reflection or *questioning insight*. He also makes the useful distinction between puzzles and problems. Puzzles have 'best' solutions and can be solved by the application of programmed knowledge with the help of experts. Problems are more complex and are dealt with by different individuals in different ways. In this context questioning insight plays a critical role. Programmed knowledge may be sought, but only after careful reflection on what knowledge is needed and why.

Action learning often takes place in small groups who come together voluntarily to work on and through their problems. This is a purposeful activity. There may be a useful cathartic element but the intention is to use the group for learning and action. Things should change in some way as a consequence. This means that people must work on real problems with which they are actively engaged, recognising that, "I am part of the problem and the problem is part of me." Each member of the group is entitled to their share of the time together and can take 20-30 minutes to talk through their issue with the group. The task of everyone else is to help this individual to check out their individual perceptions, clarify and render the problem more manageable and explore alternatives for action. It is helpful to ask good questions rather than to point out what you would do in the circumstances. It is important not to take the attention away by describing - as so often happens in normal conversation - how this situation has reminded you of an even worse one that you are facing.

The purpose is to help this individual to take action in the light of their new insight so that they can begin to change the situation. An account of the consequences will then be brought back to the group next time they meet for further shared reflection. As each individual takes their turn everyone also tries to focus on learning - not only about the problem being tackled but also on what is being learned about oneself and more generally, so that the learning might be transferred to other situations. The group needs to be aware of group processes and develop effective ways of working together. Many action learning groups have a facilitator, at least initially, whose role is to help the groups to identify and develop the necessary skills. When a group is working well it will provide the careful balance of support and challenge which enables each individual to manage more effectively. A useful metaphor in this context is that of the need of growing things for warmth and light; too much warmth and things lose their strength and start to wilt - too much light and they are shrivelled away.

Groups made up of teachers from different schools used this process to help them cope with disturbing children in their classes. All came with stories of a pupil they felt they could not manage or that they were failing in some way. They met for three hours in groups of six for five fortnightly meetings. After the first meeting almost everyone decided that they needed to carry out more careful observation of the pupil in question. Some elected to talk to a parent or colleague. Several were surprised when their observation revealed how even very young children knew how to manipulate the situation so that the teacher's attention was drawn to the 'difficult' child so that he or she - rather than anyone else - received the blame for whatever was happening. Later, people started to examine what it was in themselves that made this particular pupil difficult for them and had contributed to the breakdown in this relationship. This sharing experience did not eradicate all the problems but it enabled the teachers to stop feeling trapped in an impasse and to regain their ability to make positive changes.

One critical element of this approach to group learning is that it gives individuals legitimate time to focus on what is on their mind. Often people start by saying, "Well I don't think that I will need half an hour" and are very surprised when they do. When a group of secondary teachers on a course were given the opportunity to be part of an action learning group, several said that they could not remember the last time anyone had listened to them seriously in this way. In the busy world of schools today such important opportunities can be dismissed as self-indulgence rather than valued as the critical learning events that they can be.

A school that is full of individuals, groups and teams that are active in their learning will be well on the way to becoming a learning organisation. However, these 'hot spots' need to be aware of and linked to each other. The next chapters turn our attention to the issue of organisational learning, but the last exercise in this chapter suggests one way of linking individual, group or team learning into the whole organisation. Activity 2.6 is probably best carried out in a group but it can also be useful to think it through on your own.

Activity 2.6	I, We, They

Think of a situation that you and group colleagues would like to influence, or a change you would like to introduce that will have a impact in your school. Ask yourself:

What do I have to do to help this to happen?

What do we as a group have to do?

> [ ]

What do they (others who will be affected) have to do?

> [ ]

What can I/we do to help them to do this?

> [ ]

The answer to the third question is often very interesting. Sometimes it is surprising how little we want when it is time to be specific. The group most often identified as problematic is senior management and this can lead to some interesting thoughts or discussion about the skills of managing upwards. The last of these questions can be the most empowering. We are not helpless and hopeless. Are we giving clear enough information? Are we asking the right person the right questions? Are we so sure of the answer that we haven't even tried asking? Are we thinking of others in our organisation as colleagues? Are we open to learning from them?

CHAPTER 3

Organisational Learning

The main theme of this chapter is to continue with the theme of learning and turn attention to your school as a whole organisation and *how* an organisation learns. However, before this, the chapter provides some ways to help the process of extending an holistic understanding of your school. This, the third key characteristic of a learning school identified in Chapter 1, is perhaps the most difficult to develop. In a small school the tendency is to think in terms of individuals, and in larger schools of departments or levels in the hierarchy. These groupings are significant as we are almost certainly influenced by the nature of the groups to which we belong. It takes practice to move beyond this and to focus at the level of the whole organisation.

Developing a broader vision of this kind and thinking beyond the immediate are often cited as key leadership skills. One of the reasons often given for not appointing internal candidates for headship is that it can be difficult to take on this new perspective while remaining in the same institution. It is a particularly crucial skill for head teachers to develop and those who cannot or who choose to attempt to enhance their power through 'divide and rule' will not be enhancing organisational learning. However, this ability to think holistically should not be confined to those at the top of the hierarchy. Fullan and Hargreaves describe the dangers of:

> "a balkanised teacher culture - a culture made up of
> separate and sometimes competing groups, jockeying
> for position and supremacy like loosely connected,
> independent city states... [leading to] poor
> communication, indifference and to groups going their
> separate ways." (Fullan and Hargreaves, 1992: pp71-72)

In some schools such tendencies may be reinforced - by budget games, for example. The situation where the budget is held centrally and departments and individuals are asked to put in separate bids to be assessed by the head or a small inner circle is likely to be divisive. When there is openness, and decisions are made by a representative group asked to balance the needs of the whole student body, the process is more likely to be a unifying one. In the first case the emphasis is on individualistic thinking and on maintaining a power base. In the second, everyone is required to think beyond his or her immediate interests and in the context of the whole school.

Understanding your organisation

Where do you stand?

Activity 3.1 asks you to begin the process of thinking more holistically by considering which of the following perspectives tends to dominate your thinking. These are just six of many possible ways of focusing our attention.

Activity 3.1	The view from here

Opposite are six of the possible perspectives from which we might view education. The diagram offers two contrasting attitudes but there are obviously more possibilities.

The World
The World

The Country
The Country

Town/City/County
Town/City/County

The school
The school

My subject/class
My subject/class

Myself
Myself

Think of a major decision that your school has had to make recently:
Which perspective/s predominated?

> [blank box]

Were there any perspectives you did not consider?

> [blank box]

Can you take a different perspective? Would this have led you to the same or different conclusions?

> [blank box]

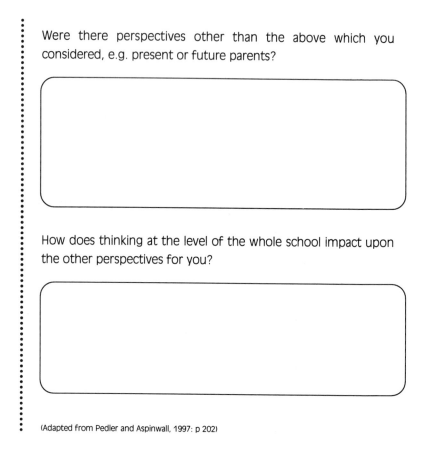

Were there perspectives other than the above which you considered, e.g. present or future parents?

How does thinking at the level of the whole school impact upon the other perspectives for you?

(Adapted from Pedler and Aspinwall, 1997: p 202)

All of the perspectives above, and others, are valid although it is likely that some will be more dominant most if not all of the time. It is difficult to hold more than one perspective at a time but each particular perspective influences decisions that you make. For example, at lunch during a programme for head teachers, one person was expounding the action he was taking to make his a more successful and effective school. He had decided to exclude any pupil who was causing a significant amount of disturbance. He described some of the pupils he had felt it necessary to exclude, ending each anecdote with the words, "So that was that. I said, 'Down the road'." After a while a fellow head leaned forward and asked, "And how does the school down the road feel about that, Gordon?"

The dominant perspective is often most apparent if you do not feel in tune with the values and approaches within your school. If, for example, you have strong pastoral and social concerns in a school with competitive academic bent, you are likely to perceive this difference as an unhelpful bias. However, this may be less apparent when you share the value position. It is not unknown for people in senior positions to assume, almost without question, that their personal preferences and the needs of 'their' school are as one.

It can be helpful, particularly before making important decisions, to make you stand back and look at a situation from some different angles. Short, medium and long term planning require a similar expansion of perspective. In the context of the learning organisation, the ability to move between perspectives is critical. Single perspective learning will always be limited in its effects, and an inability to see beyond your own or your team's immediate interests will often have wider negative effects.

What kind of school do you work in?

In Chapter 1 you were asked to think about your school in terms of metaphors. Another helpful and simple way of beginning to understand your school as a whole, as shown in Activity 3.2, is to think about the words you would use to describe it.

Activity 3.2 **What kind of place is this?**

On your own, or with a group of colleagues, each write down ten words or brief phrases that describe your school, e.g. small, untidy, hardworking, noisy, cheerful, split site, purposeful, demanding, achievement-oriented.

If you are working with others, record all of these descriptions. Indicate with ticks where more than one person uses the same word but do not rephrase or subsume.

Consider each of the words or phrases and decide whether they have positive or negative connotations, for example

+	-
hardworking	**demanding**
busy	**frantic**
stable	**static**

Now consider the implications of this for your school's approach to becoming a learning organisation, including the implications of any differences in perspective between colleagues

There are other ways of trying to capture a sense of the whole. A school is placed within a neighbourhood. It has a physical shape, a building or buildings. What is the impact of its geography? It contains pupils of different kinds and some schools are much richer in diversity in others. What do you do with this diversity: celebrate and use it to enhance learning or work to reduce it? What happens if there is little diversity in your school?

Now think about the staff. In all schools there will be a hierarchy of some kind and usually the bigger the school the more apparent this is. There may be a straightforward subject hierarchy, complicated by the fact that some people have cross school /department/year group responsibilities. In small primary schools there are often far more areas of responsibility than there are people to fill them. However, a school is also a web of social and personal relationships. It can be an interesting process to look at the conventional map of your school staff and to find ways of identifying the friendships, alliances or conflicting relationships that have a strong influence over the way things happen in the school. Try taking the formal structure of your school and use colour coding and emphasis to record the strength of the different informal relationship webs. What does this tell you about how your school works?

If you find it helpful to think graphically you could try to draw a rich picture of everyone in your school. You will need to identify what seem to be the key groups and individuals and try to place them in relationship to each other on a page. You can then try to illustrate the relationships between them. Are they separated by chasms or linked by secure bridges, for example? Is their relationship positive or negative? Do some groups have control over others? Who has most links and networks and who is isolated? Who holds out the hand of friendships and who is building up their defences? Once your picture is complete what patterns can you see? What sense can you make of the whole?

Another factor worth considering is your school's stage of development. A new school, for example, is usually a very different place to work in than a well established or declining one. Pedler, Burgoyne and Boydell (1997: pp7-8) refer to three significant factors which affect the nature of an organisation:

- the *idea* or vision which led its creation;

- the *life stage*: "Is it new, infant, pioneering, established, mature, trying to change, winding down?";

- the *era* or economic and cultural context in which it exists.

Although some schools are the creation of the churches or individuals with a particular vision of education (A.S. Neil and Summerhill being a well-known modern example), those set up by the state and the local authorities do not have individual founders. However, most of them work to establish their particular identity. What is your school most proud of - its academic success or sticking to its comprehensive ideal, or of its community link, or its willingness to get involved in innovative projects, or its prowess in particular areas, perhaps music or sport?

What is your school's life stage? Is it new or pioneering, well-established and stable, declining because of demographic and other changes, striving to regenerate and make a new start?

Whatever your answers to the above all schools are part of the same era. For better or worse, it is not the same experience to teach at the turn of the century as it was in the 1930s or the 1960s. However, you do have some choice in how you respond to the era in which you find yourself. Are you preoccupied with resisting the pressures, or are you constantly on the look out for passing bandwagons on which to leap? How much effort does your school put into understanding the current era and its effects? Does it try to influence the way things are going?

Organisational learning style

All the above factors are likely to influence your whole school's approach to learning and the processes through which it learns. The main part of this chapter offers a detailed look at one particular way of thinking about your school as a learning organisation: its organisational learning style. If individuals have personal preferences and strengths in how they learn, the same may be true for organisations. To begin thinking about what this may mean for your school, complete the questionnaire in Activity 3.3.

Activity 3.3	The Organisational Learning Styles Inventory

This questionnaire takes the form of seven incomplete sentences, each of which has five possible completing statements. For each of the incomplete sentences you have 12 points to allocate amongst the five statements depending on how typical of your school you think it is. For example, if you think that one of the five absolutely describes your school, whilst none of the other four does at all, then you could give 12 points to that one statement.

More likely you will want to distribute your 12 points amongst the five, giving most points to the one which best describes your school and few or no points to the one which least describes it.

The more you are able to discriminate, the clearer will be the Organisational Learning Style.

A. In this school, we are really good at....

1. .... operating to standard procedures ☐

2. .... collecting and storing knowledge and
   information ☐

3. .... imitating best practice in other schools ☐

4. .... innovating and finding new ways of doing things ☐

5. .... being critically aware of what is going on
   in our world ☐

Total points   12

B. The most respected people in this school are those who...

1. .... do things according to the book ☐

2. .... know a great deal about education ☐

3. .... bring in lots of new ideas from outside ☐

4. .... develop new ideas and practices on the job ☐

5. .... are always asking questions about the way
   we do things ☐

Total points   12

C. What we're most likely to say about ourselves is that we have...

1. .... very well organised systems ☐

2. .... excellent record keeping and information backup ☐

3. .... excellent networking with other schools ☐

4. .... an experimental, "leading edge" reputation ☐

5. .... wide vision and take a long view ☐

Total points 12

D. What we're least likely to say is....

1. .... "no-one sings from the same hymn sheet" ☐

2. .... "history is bunk" ☐

3. .... "we've got nothing much to learn from outsiders" ☐

4. .... "if it ain't broke, don't fix it" ☐

5. .... "go for the quick fix every time" ☐

Total points 12

E. When there's a crisis, we....

1. .... remain calm and continue with the correct procedure ☐

2. .... search for data and precedents we can learn from ☐

3. .... ring around our contacts and ask their advice ☐

4. .... drop everything else and get stuck in
   - we love it! ☐

5. .... act only after mature consideration of the
   wider implications of possible actions ☐

Total points   12

F. Our biggest weakness is...

1. .... getting stuck in fixed ways of responding ☐

2. .... depending on things which worked well for us
   in the past ☐

3. .... relying too much on other people's ideas ☐

4. .... reinventing everything - even when things
   are ticking over ☐

5. .... losing clear, short-term focus ☐

Total points   12

G. The most pressing priority for change in this school is to...

1. .... loosen up and give people more
   discretion and responsibility ☐

2. .... develop a future orientation and vision ☐

3. .... encourage people inside to develop their
   own ideas ☐

4. .... strengthen procedures and cut down on experimentation ☐

5. .... balance short and long-term foci ☐

Total points   12

Scoring
Transfer your points to the table below:-

	1	2	3	4	5
A	☐	☐	☐	☐	☐
B	☐	☐	☐	☐	☐
C	☐	☐	☐	☐	☐
D	☐	☐	☐	☐	☐
E	☐	☐	☐	☐	☐
F	☐	☐	☐	☐	☐
G	☐	☐	☐	☐	☐
Totals	☐	☐	☐	☐	☐

The five styles are described as follows:
1 = Habits
2 = Memory
3 = Imitation or Modelling
4 = Experiment
5 = Awareness or Enquiry

The higher your score for 1, 2, 3, 4 or 5 the more your organisation tends to use this style of learning according to your responses.

The lower your score for 1, 2, 3, 4 or 5 the less your organisation tends to use this style of learning according to your responses. Your score can be represented in a pie chart as shown below.

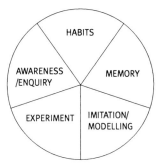

A large score for one of the five modes or styles suggests a strong preference for that way of doing things; whilst a low score indicates that this way of learning is under used. A fairly equal distribution of points could suggest that the school is balanced and multi-skilled at learning; on the other hand it might mean that it doesn't really have any learning strengths at all - it's just that you had to allocate the points somewhere!

(Pedler and Aspinwall, 1996: pp96-98)

You might like to share this questionnaire with colleagues to see how widely shared your perceptions are. It often happens that length of time in a school, role and status all have considerable influence on how things are perceived. Once you have clarified your score, read the following section, where the styles are developed in more detail.

Five organisational learning styles

Habits

These are the standard operating procedures, rules, ways of working, methods of teaching that are held onto and continue regardless of changes of staff or in the external environment. Habits are useful and can provide a crucial sense of stability. Change is disturbing for pupils as well as staff. There must be some certainties. Familiar events such as sports days, school concerts may have considerable symbolic importance and form part of the rhythm of the school year. There are aspects of the school day that are habitual. Classrooms, labs, PE lessons need a strong element of predictability and order.

Of course there is a down side to habitual behaviour. It often outlives its usefulness or becomes inappropriate. It is (sadly) not unknown for the population of a school to change quite dramatically, as its neighbourhood flourishes or declines, and yet for teachers to continue to teach in the same old way. They have learned to survive by repeating behaviour but without any emphasis on change or improvement. No one ever asks, "Why are we doing this?" Such organisations may function quite well in stable times or in protected corners of a less stable general environment.

One problem with habits is that disturbing them or even questioning their validity can threaten some core belief or sense of self. Schools are part of the collective memory and often find themselves caught up in some kind of collective romanticism, required to hold on to a better past, symbolised, perhaps by "the gold standard of A levels" or school uniforms that would not have looked out of place in the 1950s. At the same time they are being asked to prepare their pupils for the 21st century.

Memory

This term represents the stored experience of an organisation. Some of this may be in record systems but much is in the heads of individuals, largely invisible, not easily accessible and almost certainly uncollected. Sometimes important aspects of a school's memory, of past pupils and of the wider community, is held primarily in the minds of non-teaching staff - secretaries, caretakers, cleaners who often live in the community themselves and may have a long-term commitment to this particular school.

Memory differs from habit in that it does not merely reproduce the past. However, the past exerts a powerful influence over present action. A school that is strong on memory is likely to be good at monitoring, keeping records, building databases. However, an interesting aspect of memory is how much crucial knowledge about how to teach remains unspoken and unshared in schools. Little suggests that the ability to engage in "frequent, continuous and increasingly concrete and precise *talk* about practice" is a key factor in school improvement (Little, 1981: p12). We found that secondary teachers who were involved in mentoring student teachers had to learn how to be clear and explicit about practice in order to help their students (Aspinwall *et al* 1993: p100). Not only the students benefited; the teachers found that they were clarifying their own thinking and raising their own professional confidence through this process.

The downside of memory is that it can become too past-oriented and render a school strongly, and unhelpfully, resistant to change. If the school's staff is locked into cynicism, "We've seen all this before", the memory will be stifling. The balance of staffing may be crucial. The rush of early retirements caused by the change in teachers' pension arrangements wiped great swathes of memory from our schools in the late 1990s. School that have a long-term difficulty in retaining staff may be in danger of developing no useful memory at all.

Imitation/Modelling

This style involves using other schools as a benchmark and taking best practice and learning from elsewhere. This practice has long been a feature of in-service education through presentations and workshops provided by experienced practitioners. Those attending workshops often say that the opportunity to share information and ideas was the most helpful aspect of a programme. The introduction of a more competitive climate between schools may have made some more cautious about sharing information in this way but, in my experience, it has had little impact.

Local authority advisers (and in the past HMI) have seen the dissemination of good practice as a key part of their role. Visiting other institutions has also been a long established practice, with some schools attracting perhaps more attention that they can cope with. Working alongside colleagues in the same school can also provide insights into other ways of teaching or relating to particular pupils. Educationalists have also been encouraged, through grants and secondments, to spend time in the commercial sector. The ability to look outside and learn from others' experience is clearly an important skill. Fullan suggests that it is the schools that think they are self-sufficient that learn least:

> "Time and time again we find that seeking external support and training is a sign of vitality. It is the schools that act self-sufficient that are going nowhere." (Fullan, 1993: p86)

However, imitation too has its downside. There is always the danger of rushing from one flavour of the month to another, or of adopting yesterday's ideas just before their inadequacies are discovered. Processes that work well in one situation do not always transpose easily or are simply inappropriate in a different situation. Perhaps the most serious danger of all is that an institution that develops a preference for looking outside for inspiration may lose confidence in its own ability to innovate and learn.

Experiment

This learning style involves learning through innovation and trial and error. The emphasis is on trying new ways of doing things, getting feedback, reflecting and further experimentation. Experiment and innovation can be life-giving particularly when carefully paced and accompanied by reflection and evaluation. The term "ownership" is perhaps most often linked to this kind of learning and development. Sometimes more than one school may be involved in an experiment. In the past, TVEI encouraged schools and colleges to work together. Primary pyramids of schools may link up with the local secondary school. This kind of experimenting can be very creative, building on a mix of school cultures, building in ongoing review activity and checking for evidence of effectiveness.

However, unless experimentation is firmly rooted and arises out of questions relating to the fundamental purposes of a school, enthusiasm can be dangerously undirected and become mere hyperactivity. Tight budgets can make it very difficult to resource a change properly and, as one new development is overwhelmed by the next, very few reach any sort of maturity. This may suit the "change junkies" but before long most staff cease to take new initiatives seriously.

Critical awareness/Enquiry

The fifth of these learning styles is perhaps the most-wide ranging. It requires an open and questioning attitude to the organisation itself, to the wider field of education, and to the community and beyond. Everything is open to critical questioning and analysis. This kind of learning reflects Argyris and Schon's concept of double loop learning. As opposed to single loop learning, when errors are detected and corrected without any real challenge to the status quo, double loop learning requires the error or difficulty to be viewed in the wider context and may result in quite fundamental change. For example, rather than asking, "How can we do this just a little bit better?", we may have to ask, "Should we be doing this at all?" (Argyris and Schon, 1978: p3). This is difficult to do, particularly when we are investing in a new activity. Rather than there being any public acknowledgement that an initiative may have been mistaken it may just be quietly dropped. This may minimise our embarrassment but it minimises the chance of our learning from this experience even more.

This learning style is also akin to Senge's *systems thinking*, the "cornerstone" and integrating fifth discipline of the learning organisation. Unless connections, underpinning values and ultimate purposes are explored in a serious attempt to understand the whole, we are constantly frustrated by unanticipated barriers and surprised when our actions result in consequences quite different from those we intend.

There is, of course, a downside. Raising awareness can sometimes make decision-making difficult. There are so many possibilities to consider. This may lead to a loss of focus, or interest moving so far away from the day-to-day business of the school that it becomes neglected. An important element of critical awareness is to include the immediate and the here-and-now in the field of awareness.

Critical awareness requires holding on to more than one perspective at a time, being aware of short, medium and longer-term objectives. As explored in the first exercise in this chapter, a teacher will need to hold in his or her consciousness the immediacy of the classroom, within a sense of the relevant department, the whole school and the wider community. Personal needs should not be ignored, for neglect of self can lead to illness and stress. Of course, a total awareness of all these levels simultaneously is difficult, if not impossible, but remaining cocooned in a single perspective is not a viable alternative. Fullan recognises that linking schools with the wider world:

> "...requires a prodigious and mobilised effort and
> collaboration amongst a number of constituencies -
> parents and community, business and industry
> (labour and management), government and other
> social agencies, and the education system. The
> education system cannot do it alone, but it must help
> break the cycle of disjuncture by helping to lead the
> way in its own right and through alliances." (Fullan,
> 1993, p136)

All of these styles of learning are needed at different times. Some may be more essential than others at particular times or in particular situations. As with individual learning preferences, the broader and more balanced the repertoire the more learning skills a school will have to draw upon.

Although this is a pretty simple questionnaire it seems to have a high face validity for practitioners who have used it. Sometimes people are depressed by their conclusions. It is not uncommon to find someone saying, "I can tell you what we are bad at but I'm finding it very difficult to choose one of the positive statements." Teachers and heads tend to be happier with higher scores for the Experiment and Awareness/Enquiry styles. On the whole the larger the institution the larger the score for Habit and Memory.

As with all insights, the critical issue is what is now to be done.

Activity 3.4 gives you the opportunity to clarify your conclusions and identify the next steps to enable your school to enhance its learning repertoire.

Activity 3.4	Balancing and developing the school's organisational learning styles

In the light of the Organisational Learning Styles questionnaire, how well is my school developing an appropriate and healthy balance of the following learning styles:

Habits

Strength = good at forming habits and standard procedures, which survive the turnover of individuals and are important for long-term survival.

Downside = danger of unthinking repetition long after the habit has ceased to be functional - "Blind Automaton Syndrome".

Memory

Strength = good at collecting, storing and disseminating experience, knowledge and data.

Downside = can be past-oriented, relying on solutions to yesterday's problems - "Resistance to Change Syndrome".

Imitation/Modelling

Strength = good at imitating, cherry picking, benchmarking best practice internally and externally.

Downside = danger of relying too much on external ideas leading to lack of belief in ability to innovate internally - "Others Lead, We Follow Syndrome".

Experiment

Strength = good at innovation, trial and error and active experimenting with new ways of doing things.

Downside = danger of fixing what "ain't broke", of too many ideas and a preference for experiment over production - "Flavour of the Month Syndrome".

Awareness/Enquiry

Strength = good at reflecting on experience, openness and curiosity of mind; wide awareness of the school, other parts of the education system and the wider environment.

Downside = danger of losing focus, lack of attention to detail, difficulty in making decision - "Ivory Tower Syndrome".

Summary

"In terms of organisational learning, in my organisation we are...

1. .... best at: (i) _____

and next best at (ii) _____

2. .... worst at: (i) _____

and next worst at (ii) _____

3. .... most endangered by the "_____ Syndrome"

4. .... most in need of _____ to improve learning in the organisation.

5. .... Our next step will be to _____

(Based on Pedler and Aspinwall, 1996: pp96-99)

CHAPTER 4

Schools as Learning Organisations

This chapter opens by addressing a fundamental issue: that of purpose. It asks you to think about your school's underpinning values and the principles that will guide you in becoming a learning organisation. It then looks in some detail at two particular models: The 11 Characteristics of the Learning Organisation and the Energy Flow Model and how these can be used to relate to your organisation. It concludes with a process to help identify the main features of a learning school.

What is the learning for?

When learning becomes so important, deeper questions are inevitably raised:

- What is all this learning for?
- What do we want to be as a school?
- If we want to better than we are now, what does "better" mean?

When we are busy and under pressure we are often preoccupied with the *what* and the *how*; in this context - what is a learning organisation and how do we become one? We are anxious to action, to get on with what needs to be done. The question of implementation is an important and critical focus. However, an exclusive focus on the *how* can lead us to become blinkered and to cease questioning the purpose of what we are doing. The organisation or person blinded by a vision no longer asks the *why*?

question; "the Blind Automaton" can be a dangerous beast which unknowingly crushes everything in its path.

The need to learn is always connected with the fundamental purposes of an organism. As individual human beings, or as groups or teams of people, we learn in order to get on with life in the best way we can. Any radical attempt to change what we are doing resurfaces the questions of identity, of purpose, of mission. The *why?* questions take us into the wider context. How do we fit in with the whole? What is our part? How do we make sense of what we're doing?

Schooling cannot be value neutral. Three factors make the need for a moral basis for what we do compelling:

- Education is compulsory, and for most children this means going to school

- Those in receipt of this compulsory process are children

- Education is for the most part a public service funded by all out of taxation.

Fullan (1993: p4) places great emphasis on this:

> "Education has a moral purpose. The moral purpose
> is to make a difference in the lives of students
> regardless of background and to help produce citizens
> who can live and work productively in increasingly
> dynamically complex societies."

He quotes the moral requirements listed by Sirotnik (1990: p298):

> "inquiry, knowledge, competence, caring, freedom,
> well-being and social justice"

Essential as these are at the classroom level, Fullan reminds us that we must go beyond this to think of what these moral requirements mean in the wider context, and to recognise that teachers cannot do all that is necessary on their own.

The core fundamental purpose of a school must be to meet the needs of its pupils. This can have its complications, for example, the needs of pupils may appear conflicting. However, these difficulties have to be managed. Consider the following analogy which Will Hutton uses to contrast the income distribution within the population of the UK:

> "If the population of Britain were divided according
> to income, if income were made equivalent to height
> and if the population then marched past for an hour,
> it would take a full 37 minutes before the first adult of
> average height was seen. For the first 15 minutes
> there would be a parade of dwarves. Stature would
> increase gradually thereafter, but 57 minutes would
> have to pass before we saw people of twice the
> average height. Giants of 90 feet or more would
> appear in the last few seconds, with the last one or
> two literally miles high." (Hutton, 1995: p193)

Supposing you were to try to develop a similar picture of the attention paid to differing groups of pupils in your school. It is very unlikely that there will be anything like this degree of contrast but would all your pupils be of the same height? Which groups are disadvantaged and why? Now apply the same thinking to the children and young people in your wider community. What are the differences? What part does your school play in this?

We need to look both within and without if a school is to ensure that its organisational learning is taking it in the right direction. The learning school must have strong connections with the community and the world outside the school. Schooling is a public service. It is not the exclusive property of its staff or of its current pupils and their parents. Its purposes must of necessity include the longer term if it is to fulfil the purpose of developing future citizens and preparing them to cope with adult life.

Who are the people who have a direct or indirect interest in the purpose of your school. How much do you know about their aspirations? Try to clarify your thoughts through Activity 4.1.

Activity 4.1 — Stakeholder analysis

The purpose of this activity is to identify those who have a stake in your school, and to consider what part they can play in helping you to clarify the fundamental purpose of your organisation. A stakeholder is any individual or group who is affected by, or can affect the future of, your school. Ask yourself:

- Who has an interest in our school?
- Who can affect what we do and how we do it?
- Who can express an opinion?
- Who ought to or might care about it?

Identify both internal and external stakeholders, present and future, and place them in the columns below:

Internal Stakeholders	View of Core Purposes	External Stakeholder	View of Core Purposes

How easy did you find it to identify the view of the school's core purposes held by each of these individuals or groups?

When did you last check this with them?

Can you prioritise this list?

How widely shared will your view of these priorities be?

What are the implications of your answers?

(Adapted from Aspinwall et al, 1992: p89)

The fact that a school needs to be in tune with its community does not mean that it must, therefore, be a prisoner to the vagaries of public opinion. If there is meaningful communication with the people that matter, there will be meaningful and learning-full debate about what the school is for. The sealed, inward looking school will have no chance of influencing wider perceptions and will be unlikely to develop the kind of awareness needed in a learning school aiming for a sustainable future.

It can be hard to hold on to a sense of moral purpose and agency in the pressure for efficiency, effectiveness, targets and results, "crushed", as Stephen Ball so graphically puts it, "in the nexus between managerialism and the market"(Ball, 1994: p62). Means and ends become confused and short-term reaction takes precedence over considering longer-term consequences. Holding on to the question, "What is the learning for?", as set out in Activity 4.2, may provide some kind of an anchor. It does not deny the immediate pressures but may help you lift your head at least a little beyond them.

Activity 4.2 | **What is this learning for: The How/Why Ladder**

Why do you aspire to become a learning organisation? Can you complete the How /Why ladder for your school.

The Learning School
Purpose - What does our school stand for?

and Why?

How might we move forward?

Action: what next step will we take?

Two models of the learning organisation

Having clarified your school's core purpose and values you will be ready to move on and to set your school into the contexts of the next two models, which are taken from *The Learning Company* by Pedler, Burgoyne and Boydell. The first is the 11 Characteristics of a Learning Organisation, which provides an approach to inform your planning processes. The second is the Energy Flow Model, which is designed to explore how the energy of learning and information flow around an organisation when it is working well as a whole.

The 11 Characteristics of the Learning Organisation

Pedler, Burgoyne and Boydell (1997: pp15-17) have collected together the characteristics found in common among organisations that are aspiring to become learning organisations. Much of their information is drawn from commercial companies and public services other than schools but the characteristics are also relevant to schools. Whilst these descriptions do not refer to any actual school they can serve as a useful template against which to make comparisons. The 11 characteristics they have identified are as follows.

1. A learning approach to strategy

Development of policy and strategy is consciously structured for learning purposes - for example, new approaches will be piloted and then thoughtfully evaluated, and small scale experiments will be used to create feedback loops for learning about effectiveness and what should happen next.

Such approaches have been relatively rare in the last few years when generic "solutions" have been imposed in a variety of different situations one after the other with little evident regard for evaluation. This makes the need for a learning approach to strategy inside a school even more urgent if you are not to feel helplessly tossed on the flood of initiatives.

2. Participative policy making

All or most members of the organisation have a chance to contribute and participate in making policy. Ideally they do this together with other key stakeholders so that policy reflects and supports a diversity of ideas.

The amount of participation ordinary teachers have in making policy varies a great deal. Bottery (1992: p51) distinguishes three types of involvement: "pseudo participation" where staff are persuaded to accept decisions already made by management; "partial participation", where staff can genuinely influence decisions; and, exceptionally, "full participation" where each person has equal power to determine the outcome. Much the same range of difference is found amongst stakeholders. In schools the board of governors can play an important role in representing key stakeholders, but in addition it is important to consider whether all groups are truly represented and how best they might participate.

3. Informating

In the learning organisation information technology is not just about automation but is used to inform people about critical aspects of the business in order to encourage and empower them to act on their own initiative.

This term is applied here to the use of information technology but obviously has wider implications. Schools need to be able to understand, grapple with and make use of the plethora of statistics and information surrounding them. For example, test and exam results and league tables can be used as indicators to be explored, understood and used for future planning, or as mechanisms to divide and punish.

4. Formative accounting and control
This is a particular aspect of informating, where systems of budgeting, reporting and accounting are structured to assist learning in all members about how money works in the organisation.

The tasks of budgeting and accounting have taken an increasingly high profile in schools in recent years. The proper and careful management of public money to the greater good of pupils is obviously an important task. But budgetary control should not be an end in itself. The distribution of the budget can be organised to enhance the reward power of a few individuals or to spread information, decision making and learning around the organisation.

5. Internal exchange
There is a high degree of internal exchange, learning from other departments is normal, with staff tending to see themselves as fellow learners or as customers of and suppliers to each other.

The value to teachers of talking and learning together has been referred to in Chapter 1.

6. Reward Flexibility
Greater autonomy and empowerment for staff leads to a need for more flexible rewards. Here there is flexibility in both monetary and non-monetary rewards to cater for individual needs and performance.

There is little leeway in schools for flexibility in financial reward and concern, for example, about possible negative effects of any proposals to pay "good" teachers more than their colleagues. However, money is not the only motivator and there may be more creative and more mutual ways of rewarding excellence.

7. Enabling structures

A wide concept covering all aspects of roles, processes and procedures - seen as temporary structures, easily changed to meet job or customer requirements.

Many schools have long-established and relatively rigid structures, which can lead to problems when, for example, the parameters of subject departments are redrawn.

8. Boundary workers as environmental scanners

Environmental scanning is carried out by people who have contacts with the outside world of users, suppliers, business partners, neighbours and so on. Processes for bringing back and disseminating information in the organisation are also important.

To take just one relevant group as an example, teachers often come into direct and regular contact with parents, in particular, but do not always use this contact effectively. In one school, staff declared that all parents fell into one of two distinct categories: either over-anxious or indifferent. They could not see the parents as a resource nor could they hear any of the quite valid questions that these parents were raising. Responding to the requirements of parents who do not have easy daily contact with a school is a problem for even the best-intentioned school. What mechanisms do you have in place for keeping in touch?

9. Inter-company learning

The organisation meets with others for mutual exchange and learning through benchmarking, joint ventures and other alliances.

Schools have traditionally looked to other schools as sources of ideas and have come into contact with other teachers through INSET and LEA meetings and conferences.

10. A learning climate

A good learning climate is one where leaders and managers facilitate their own and other people's experimentation and learning from experience, through questioning, feedback and support.

Schools vary in their learning climate. In some it is possible - even encouraged - to share and discuss both triumphs and difficulties; in others lack of trust or the maintenance of a myth of competence makes openness very difficult.

11. Self-development opportunities for all

This involves making resources and facilities for self-development available to all members of the organisation and not just the favoured few.

Managing this can be difficult for schools with a limited staff development budget and may involve a more creative approach to development than a focus on courses.

(Pedler, Burgoyne and Boydell, 1997: pp 15-17)

My school and The 11 Characteristics of the Learning Company

How does your school measure up to The 11 Characteristics of the Learning Company ? You can think about this alone, of course, but it is far better to involve other people in the exercise, for then you have the opportunity to discuss where you agree and disagree - which is the best way of making the use of this sort of model. You can do this by distributing this questionnaire as a survey to all the people in a team, department or whole school, collect the anonymous replies, score them and then feed them back as a way of starting a discussion on this topic. This might lead to some good ideas for improving the learning in your school.

| Activity 4.3 | The 11 Characteristics of the Learning Company questionnaire |

Give your organisation a score out of 5 for each of the statements listed below. Giving 5 points to any statement would mean that your organisation is very much like this; a score of 0 or 1 would suggest that it is not much, or never, like this.

1. We regularly examine the social, economic, political and wider trends that affect our school.

2. Everyone here plays a part in policy and strategy formation. ☐

3. Access to organisational information and databases is open to all. ☐

4. The financial consequences of actions are fed back to those concerned as soon as they are known. ☐

5. Departments and year groups etc. understand each other's purposes and values. ☐

6. There are many different ways of rewarding good work, monetary and non-monetary. ☐

7. Structures are very flexible and change frequently to suit different tasks and purposes. ☐

8. People routinely bring in and share information about what's happening out there from parents, community, local employers and so on. ☐

9. We engage in joint ventures to develop new approaches and to learn about new methods and ideas. ☐

10. People are not blamed for raising bad news. ☐

11. Everyone is encouraged to learn new skills and abilities. ☐

12. We find new directions by experimenting with practice and by setting up pilot projects. ☐

13. Important policies are widely discussed before they are adopted. ☐

14. Information technology really
helps us to do new things together. □

15. People understand the importance of money
and resources and also how such things work
in this organisation. □

16. Different departments and sections share
information and skills and help each other
out as a matter of course. □

17. Most people have a say in the nature and
shape of reward systems. □

18. People are encouraged to come up with different
ways of organising work. □

19. There are effective channels of communication
for collecting and sharing information from
outside the school. □

20. We often meet with other schools or relevant
organisations to share ideas and practices. □

21. The central focus of our appraisals is the
exploration of the person's learning and
development needs. □

22. There are many opportunities, materials and
resources available for everyone's learning on an
"open access" basis. □

Scoring
Now find your scores by adding the responses to two questions
for each of The 11 Characteristics of the Learning Company.
For example, Characteristic 1 - A Learning Approach to Strategy -
is scored by adding together the points for Q 1 + Q 12.

Totals

1. A Learning Approach to   add Q 1 + Q 12 =   [ ]
   Strategy

2. Participative Policy Making   add Q 2 + Q 13 =   [ ]

3. Informating   add Q 3 + Q 14 =   [ ]

4. Formative Accounting and   add Q 4 + Q 15 =   [ ]
   Control

5. Internal Exchange   add Q 5 + Q 16 =   [ ]

6. Reward Flexibility   add Q 6 + Q 17 =   [ ]

7. Enabling Structures   add Q 7 + Q 18 =   [ ]

8. Boundary Workers as   add Q 8 + Q 19 =   [ ]
   Environmental Scanners

9. Inter-company Learning   add Q 9 + Q 20 =   [ ]

10. A Learning Climate   add Q 10 + Q 21 =   [ ]

11. Self-development   add Q 11 + Q 22 =   [ ]
    Opportunities for All

Analysis

Looking at the scores, what do you see? Typically there will be a range of scores, with the organisation scoring higher on some items than on others. This is where it is useful to have some discussion in order to make sense of what these scores may mean. Do these high and low scores represent your strengths and weaknesses as a learning organisation? Are there weaknesses that you would like to improve on or strengths that you wish to build up further?

Dissatisfaction index

How would you like your school to be? You could do the questionnaire a second time asking yourself, if this is how it is at the moment, how would I like it to be in future? This second set of scores will provide a "gap analysis", which, in effect, prioritises the 11 Characteristics of the Learning Company as far as your school is concerned. From these two scores a *dissatisfaction index* can be calculated:

$$\text{Dissatisfaction Index} = 100 \times \frac{\text{How it should be - How it is}}{\text{How it should be}}$$

If people are totally dissatisfied, this index will be 100. If they are completely satisfied with things as they are, then it is zero. Of course the next step is to decide what action seems appropriate in the particular circumstances of your school.

The next model is very different and at first sight may appear more difficult to understand but it is helpful in understanding how an organisation works.

The Energy Flow Model

This model is based on the idea that for an organisation to work well it needs to maximise the way that energy and learning flows throughout. It proposes that there are four necessary functions at the heart of any organisation (see Figure 4.1):

- **Policy (P)** or the underpinning purpose, including values and vision i.e. "What does this school stand for?"

- **Operations (O)** or the structures, systems and approaches that enable this purpose to become a reality i.e. "How does this school work?"

- **Action (A)** or the action in which individuals are engaged i.e. "What are individuals actually doing?"

- **Ideas (I)** or the ideas and beliefs which individuals bring to their work i.e. "What do individuals think and believe?"

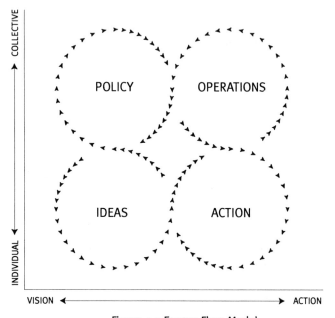

Figure 4.1 Energy Flow Model

Together these four functions produce four double feedback loops representing different types of energy, information and learning. In this model:

- The continuous flow back and forth between the *Policy* and *Operations* loops at the top of the diagram is the *collective* or corporate learning cycle

- The continuous flow between *Ideas* and *Action* and vice versa is the *individual* or personal learning cycle

- The *Policy* and *Ideas* loop is concerned with inner thoughts, ideas and intentions at the individual or organisational level

- The *Operations* and individual *Action* loop is the outer, action-orientated part of what goes on in your school.

For an organisation to work and learn effectively, energy must flow through and link all of these functions. A school will need to balance the four key functions, otherwise individuals may pull against each other, and structures and systems may impede rather than promote the school's fundamental purposes. The process is interrupted and prevented by:

- *biases*, when any one, two or three of these processes predominate to the exclusion or disadvantage of the others, and

- *blocks*, where a function exists but is disconnected from, and uninfluenced by, the others.

For example, if a school is biased towards just two of these functions, e.g. **I** - individual ideas and **A** - individual actions, teachers would tend to work alone in their classrooms pursuing their own interests. Any time together would be spent on non-educational matters such as fund raising, gossip or practical matters. A school that is biased towards **P** and **O** would be following a detailed syllabus, teaching to a prescribed format with no room for individual preference and initiative. The combination of a bias towards **O** and **A** would be a school caught up in activity with no reflection and no shared sense of purpose; and **P** and **I** would lead to endless planning and reflection with no action at all. Such extreme biases are rare but three way biases may be more familiar. For example:

IA pO	the lack of a policy dimension which would leave a school lacking in any real sense of direction or purpose.
IA Po	a school lacking any collective organisational function. This might suit a group of autonomous, dynamic and creative people happy to work around a set of policies or

principles but might prove confusing and disconnected for the pupils. Some primary schools in the UK were able to carry on quite comfortably in this way before the advent of the national curriculum.

iA
PO

allowing no room for the influence of individual ideas (perhaps appropriate for a cult or an army engaged in conflict) might serve in a moment of crisis but would be unlikely in the longer term to attract committed professionals to work in a school.

Ia
PO

because of the nature of schooling it is hard to envisage the absence of any individual action except in the context of a proposed new development. In this case ideas, structures and processes might be designed and redesigned by a team but never be put into action and become a reality.

Identifying the blocks to the smooth flow of energy between the four functions is also illuminating. For example:

- Two education officers from Zimbabwe realised that in many instances the policy function felt quite disconnected from the other three. This was because many initiatives were funded from abroad and therefore reflected the policies and priorities of the funders rather than of the Zimbabweans.

- Tutors from a College of Nursing realised that, because the operations function was by far the dominant bias in their organisation, individual ideas tended to be blocked from influencing both individual action and the development of policy.

- A primary teacher realised that her school was still in the process of learning how to develop the policy function and to link it to individual ideas. The initial response of her head teacher to the need to produce a School Development Plan had been to write one single-handed. However, now there was a real attempt being made to involve all staff and bring their individual ideas into the process.

- A different form of block is quite common in secondary schools where there may be barriers or perhaps a lack of means or systems to enable communication between the operational tunnels of subject departments. Teachers who undertake to track individual pupils through their day are often disturbed to find some issues covered several times in different subject areas while others are nowhere to be found. They also find pupils moving from one lesson to another to be presented with the same teaching technique in each.

How does the energy flow around these functions in your school? Consider this in Activity 4.4, which follows on p90.

Activity 4.4 — The energy flow activity

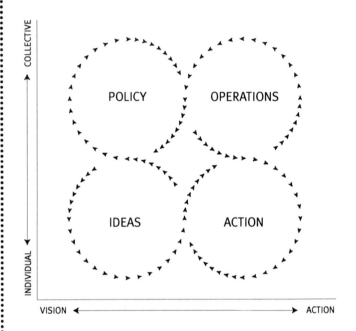

Energy Flow Model

Take either a blue pencil or 20 of the blue sticky spots that you can buy in a stationers and indicate on the energy flow diagram above your estimate of the current distribution of energy and learning in your organisation.

Then take 5 red spots or a red pen and add them to the diagram to show where you would like to see energy increased.

Now ask yourself:
Where is the energy and learning strongest in my organisation?

Are these particular biases helpful or not?

Where is the energy blocked and why?

What seems to be working well and why?

What steps might I and others take to improve this situation?

(Pedler, Burgoyne and Boydell, 1996: pp 39-43)

This model may also be used to consider the balance of the four processes (directing, managing, learning and participating) that are linked to the positive connections between each of the pairs below:

Policy (P) ¤ *Operations* (O) = Directing
Operations (O) ¤ *Action* (A) = Managing
Action (A) ¤ *Ideas* (I) = Learning
Ideas (I) ¤ *Policy* (P) = Participating

Directing is akin to leadership, providing the steer and sense of purpose. Managing ensures that purpose becomes reality and that reality feeds back and influences policy and purpose. Ideas and actions link together to bring about learning. Individual ideas both influence and are influenced by the development of policy, leading to active participation and commitment at all levels in the school. These processes are needed at all levels within an organisation. A school that is divided into those who direct and those who do not will not be effective at organisational learning.

The four processes are often not equally well developed. For most organisations, participating seems to be the most problematic. A head teacher working with this model reflected:

> "I realise that I have considered myself to be very
> consultative. But what I actually do is invite the staff
> into my office regularly to talk to me as individuals.
> Then I decide what the general view in the school is
> on any particular issue. I am going to try to work
> more openly with the whole staff so that we can
> decide some issues together."

While this model is particularly useful as a framework for examining the effectiveness of internal processes, it is also necessary to consider the organisation in its wider context. The world outside the school will impinge on each of the four functions in different ways. For example, government policy in the UK has increasingly affected the way in which schools work. Schools are required to put specified policies into action. The National

Curriculum has strongly influenced the operational function. Individual teachers may live and take action in their local communities or bring in ideas from national bodies or their own developmental activities. These and many other influences come in and contribute to the flow of organisational energy and learning.

Here too there may be biases and blocks. For example, teachers often express frustration and disappointment when new ideas and fresh energy gained from courses fall upon stony ground on their return to school. Policies in themselves change little and are often undermined or "translated", particularly when they are imposed from outside and there can have been no participation in their creation. In these situations, far from external influences increasing the energy flow, precious energy is wasted on resistance.

Making use of the Energy Flow Model requires setting it into context. The four functions may be influenced by the size of a school and the age group served. However, checking the flow of energy, identifying biases and blockages, developing strategies to overcome these can lead to a significant growth in both energy and learning within a school.

Defining your learning school

By using Activity 4.5 try to put together the various ideas that have been presented to you and draw up your design for a learning school. What do you perceive to be the significant features? What would you want to see in place?

Activity 4.5	Defining your learning school

You can do this alone, but it is better in the company of a few other people.

1. First of all, brainstorm how your school would be - what it

would look like, feel like, and **HOW WOULD IT ACT** - if it was a learning organisation.

Write your ideas or statements on post-its and stick them up on a flipchart or wall.

2. Now forget about your ideal picture for the time being and brainstorm your idea of a NON-learning school.

You can have some fun here by recalling all the situations you have been in where learning was avoided, prevented or crushed, where mistakes were covered up, where people were blamed for speaking the truth, rewarded for resisting innovation and so on.

As before, write your ideas or statements on Post-its and stick them up on a flipchart or wall.

3. Now look at both sets of statements - what must and what must not be there in your ideal learning organisation? Sort your Post-its into these three groups:

MUST	**COULD**	**MUST NOT**
be there	**be there**	**be there**

Sometimes visions are easier to arrive at by deciding what you don't want as much as by what you would want to see there. These are the "noxiants" - poisons which will kill off your vision before it can be realised.

4. Finally tidy up your MUST list (including any COULDs you want) to complete the following sentence in as few words as possible whilst capturing your key ideas or statements:

"In _____ (Your school's name) what we mean by the learning organisation is _____

Now that you have a vision, you can begin to bring it about and look for ways of enhancing learning for individuals and for the organisation as a whole.

CHAPTER 5

What Gets in
the Way of Learning?

The fact that the idea of creating a learning school is attractive does not make it easy to achieve. The best of intentions can be thwarted and in some difficult situations good intentions may themselves be difficult to find. The learning organisation has to be generated from within, starting with the aims and aspirations of the people concerned. It may inspire some people to become excited and anxious to push ahead. Enthusiasm can be attractive (and is certainly preferable to apathy) but it can generate its own problems. It is important to acknowledge from the outset that all-powerful visions have downsides or shadows and that these can affect the very best of efforts. When starting out bravely on a quest it is as well to know about the pitfalls along the way. What will we do when things don't turn out as planned?

When caught up in a difficult situation, people often focus on individuals or groups as the cause of the problem. They can say (or think), "If only the head wouldn't...", "That's so typical of X...", "Nothing creative ever comes out of that department..." Instead they could be thinking at the level of the whole organisation. Sometimes problems can be attached to particular individuals who manifest much the same kind of behaviour no matter where they are or who they work with or for. But much of our behaviour is influenced by our situation, with certain conditions bringing out the best or the worst in us. As we know, some schools seem to create more pupils that need to be excluded than others. Working in an LEA advisory service for several years enabled me to see teachers who had struggled in one situation flourish in another and vice versa. The organisational context quite clearly made a difference. This is why it can be so helpful to think at the level of the whole.

What is it that influences behaviour? What encourages individuals, teams and departments to learn? And what stops, prevents or inhibits learning?

This chapter looks at common problems in schools and other organisations. It starts by considering just how bad things might be and ends with the problems of a school where the problem is not too much negativity but where there is too great an impulse to agree.

Organisations have their own cultures and climates and some of these are more enhancing or more damaging than others. All organisations also have their shadow side and this theme will be explored at the end of the chapter. There are, however, some schools that are in such an unhappy state that any creativity and commitment that emerges is somehow poisoned before it can develop. Such organisations can be described as toxic. This is an unpleasant description but it does help to capture the sense of a place where, as in a heavily polluted forest, little can flourish. Consider this in Activity 5.1.

Activity 5.1	The organisational toxicity index (OTI)

For each of the following 10 statements choose one of the responses, (a), (b) or (c), to indicate which is truest of your school, in your experience, for most of the time.

In my organisation ...
1. ...sexist and racist remarks are commonplace and widely tolerated.

(a) This is not a problem.

(b) This is something of a problem.

(c) This is a big problem for me and others.

2. ...praise is much rarer than criticism.

(a) This is not a problem. ☐

(b) This is something of a problem. ☐

(c) This is a big problem for me and others. ☐

3. ...you get little information about your own performance.

(a) This is not a problem. ☐

(b) This is something of a problem. ☐

(c) This is a big problem for me and others. ☐

4. ...there is competitive pressure from other staff to work long hours.

(a) This is not a problem. ☐

(b) This is something of a problem. ☐

(c) This is a big problem for me and others. ☐

5. ...there is little concern shown for members' health and welfare.

(a) This is not a problem. ☐

(b) This is something of a problem. ☐

(c) This is a big problem for me and others. ☐

6. ...making admissions of mistakes or failure is "career limiting".

(a) This is not a problem. ☐

(b) This is something of a problem. ☐

(c) This is a big problem for me and others. ☐

7. ...all management decisions are justified in terms of the "bottom line" i.e. solely on financial grounds.

(a) This is not a problem. ☐

(b) This is something of a problem. ☐

(c) This is a big problem for me and others. ☐

8. ...there are a lot of hierarchical distinctions.

(a) This is not a problem. ☐

(b) This is something of a problem. ☐

(c) This is a big problem for me and others. ☐

9. ...there is little diversity in the senior management team - most are male and white.

(a) This is not a problem. ☐

(b) This is something of a problem. ☐

(c) This is a big problem for me and others. ☐

10. …it's very hard to get people to listen to you and your ideas.

(a) This is not a problem. ☐

(b) This is something of a problem. ☐

(c) This is a big problem for me and others. ☐

Scoring
Score 0 for every (a) 1 for every (b) and 2 for every (c).
The minimum score is 0, the maximum 20.

If you scored less than 5, then your organisation is comparatively healthy, although there may be some points that need attention.

If you scored 6 to 12, then your organisation is quite toxic - to the point that many people's performance must be impaired.

If you scored more than 12, your organisation is getting to the point where it is not fit for staff or pupils to live and work in.

(Adapted from Pedler, Burgoyne and Boydell, 1997: pp153-154)

Hopefully your results will not be too depressing. Whatever the score, it is interesting to consider where these characteristics come from. If your organisation is truly toxic it is likely that energy will be spent in looking for someone on whom to lay the blame. But if your aspiration is to learn you will be more likely to ask, "What part do I play in this process? What does our team contribute? What can be done to change the situation?"

Learning disabilities in organisations

Peter Senge (1990: pp18-25) suggests that almost all organisations experience problems in ensuring that learning takes place. He describes these as learning disabilities and identifies the seven which he has found to be the most common:

1. *"I Am My Position"* The situation in which someone manifests a narrow focus on "my" job rather than on the shared purpose of the whole. In some schools position is very important. In one a new member of staff was advised, "You must be careful not to tread on anybody's toes - and some people around here have very big feet."

2. *"The Enemy Is Out There"* Here everyone blames everyone else or a particular group or the LEA or the government or ... when things go wrong. The question, "How do we contribute to the problem?" will not be asked.

3. *"The Illusion of Taking Charge"* Human beings generally like to feel that they are in control. However, quite often "taking charge" is in reality a reaction to what is being asked or imposed rather than true proactiveness or a real choice of direction. Rapid response rather than thoughtful consideration becomes the order of the day.

4. *"The Fixation on Events"* This leads to a preoccupation with the fine details of short-term events without looking at the wider context which may be the actual source of the difficulty. This in turn means that notice is not taken of the slow gradual processes such as ...

5. *"The Parable of the Boiled Frog"* The rather gruesome analogy in which the water is brought so slowly to the boil that the danger is not recognised and the frog lapses into sleep and dies instead of leaping to safety.

6. *"The Delusion of Learning from Experience"* Here, learning from experience is not guaranteed. The meaning of a particular experience and the unintended consequences of actions are not always apparent. Another common way of expressing this learning disability is the observation that while one person has

had 20 years' experience, another has had one year of experience repeated 20 times.

7. *"The Myth of the Management Team"* Many "teams" prefer to maintain the appearance of cohesion rather than face up to and deal positively with internal differences. This makes them much more prone to falling apart under pressure.

Can you identify with any of these disabilities? Are they manifest in you school? Have you developed collectively any other significant ones of your own? These learning disabilities are made worse when we are stuck in a reactive stance to changes coming from outside rather than generating a personal vision of where we want to be and how we are going to get there. But what causes these learning disabilities? Senge (1990: p52) suggests three levels of explanation in any system:

- Level 1:   *Events*   (Reactive)

  If we see things in terms of isolated events we are likely to be reactive and to blame other people or groups for what has gone wrong.

- Level 2:   *Patterns of behaviour*   (Responsive)

  If we understand things in terms of patterns of behaviour this enables us to become more thoughtful and responsive to trends, avoiding the reactiveness trap.

- Level 3:   *Systemic structure*   (Generative)

  This is the deepest level, involving feedback loops and delays, spirals and cycles leading to the realisation that no one person is to blame, the problem is a joint production made up of many individual actions. There are clear links here to Pedler, Burgoyne and Boydell's levels of organisational learning identified in Chapter 1.

Organisational politics

There are different attitudes to organisational politics: some people would prefer to deny their existence, others to hold themselves above them and others seem to thrive on them. Gerard Egan suggests that organisational politics exist wherever there are people and groups who:

- enjoy the use of power;

- vie for scarce resources;

- protect their own "turf";

- have different ideologies and values;

- compete with others to "win" battles.

(Egan, 1993: pp 111-115)

It would be unusual not to find these factors in your school, although each may be pursued more or less aggressively. All organisations are political to a greater or lesser extent, but this can of course work either to enhance or damage organisational effectiveness. Political activity clearly impacts on the organisation's ability to learn and will affect any learning organisation strategy.

Baddeley and James (1987) provide a helpful model for thinking about this aspect of organisational life. They have found that individuals have contrasting ways of *reading* any situation they enter. Some are acutely politically aware; others are unaware and simple do not notice this dimension. Some see organisational life as an arena for playing psychological games whilst others place value on behaving with integrity. Combined, these two dimensions provide a useful model or framework for thinking (see Figure 5.1). There are four corners in which to place yourself and your colleagues. You may be politically aware and into game playing, in which case you are *clever* and a *fox*; politically unaware but into game playing i.e. *inept* and a *donkey*; politically unaware but wanting to act with integrity - *innocent* and a *sheep*; or politically aware and acting with integrity - *wise* and an *owl*.

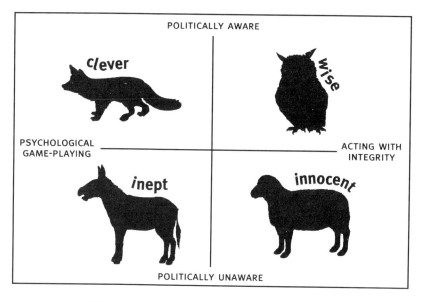

(Baddeley and James, 1987)

Figure 5.1 Four political responses

This model can be particularly helpful to those who avoid being political because they assume that it is impossible to retain their personal integrity and do so. Sheep-like behaviour is both personally and organisationally unhelpful. Teachers who refuse to take note of the political dimension will be surprised by and ill-prepared for what happens and may find that they, their pupils and the things they care about are damaged in the process. Wise owls know where the power lies, what needs to be done and how to work with and enhance both the formal and informal systems, and they are straight forward and open about their behaviour and do not compromise their beliefs. Few people would aspire to be donkeys or engage in inept behaviour. Feelings about being fox-like may be more mixed. Some foxes may be masquerading as owls by convincing themselves that the end justifies the means or that they are being acute rather than manipulative. It is certainly more difficult to be an owl - and more dangerous to be a sheep - in an organisation pervaded by fox-like behaviour, particularly where this is the dominant mode amongst senior managers.

When using this model it is worth noting two things. Firstly, it is most useful to apply it to behaviour in specific circumstance. Some people may be fixed into one or other of these corners but most of us can find ourselves in any one of these positions in different circumstances. As an extension of this, try to identify the interface you move between most frequently. Do you hover between ineptness and cleverness, cleverness and wisdom, wisdom and innocence or innocence and ineptness? A learning organisation that is at the survival or reactive stage could be either clever or wise, but wisdom becomes essential to achieve sustainability.

The problem of time

Recently two teachers who had not met for several years were discussing the way work now seemed to dominate their lives. They agreed that they had always felt busy but never quite so frenzied and pulled in all directions. In trying to understand the difference, one suggested that in the past "being busy" had included spending time in planning and thinking whereas now, the pressure is about being engaged in endless action.

Although spending time on developing vision, mission and values is becoming a more familiar part of development programmes, that vision becomes dimmed by relentless demands for things to be done when limitations and constraints (often time and money) make the vision seem impossible to attain. There is ever less time to distinguish the wood from the trees. Incessant action allows no moment to pause, take stock and set some priorities.

One practical step you can take when thinking about the balance between your vision and reality, is to reflect in Activity 5.2 on the degree of choice and discretion that you actually have.

Activity 5.2 Demands, Choices and Constraints

All activity can be analysed in terms of:

Constraints - Things that you must live with, e.g. finance, legislation, professional boundaries, policies, timetables, and above all, time.

Demands - Things you must do, expectations you must meet.

Choices - Things about which you have some control or say over what to do (or not to do), how to do it, how much and when.

The relationships between these can be drawn diagrammatically. For example:

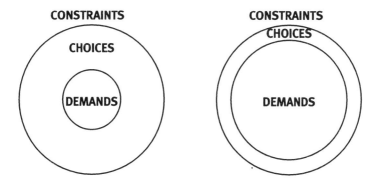

Either on your own or in a group, draw your own chart, thinking carefully about the area of choice available to you. Distinguishing between choices, demands and constraints can be more a matter of personal judgement and assumption than at first appears. It is useful to review whether you are using choice to become more "busy", for example and to ask, "Who am I trying to please?"

Choices

Write down the main areas of choice open to you within your job. How well are you handling these?

(a) I am clear about how much choice I have.

clear 1   2   3   4   5   unclear

(b) The choices I make help me to function more effectively.

agree 1   2   3   4   5   disagree

(c) The choices I make enable me to manage pressure well.

agree 1   2   3   4   5   disagree

Is it possible for you to manage your area of choice more effectively?

Demands

Now list the principal demands. Can any of these be challenged by asking:
- Why does this have to be done?
- How important is it?
- Exactly how much is needed?
- Can it be done more efficiently or effectively?

Constraints

Now list, reflect on, and challenge your constraints.
- Are you clear about their exact nature or are you assuming that things are worse than they really are?
- Are there any areas of flexibility?
- Is there anything that can be done to change any of these constraints?
- Are any of these constraints actually helpful?

Return to your original diagram. Do you need to make any changes?

(Based on Stewart, 1982: pp2-10)

Mandated change and innovation fatigue

A different kind of explanation of what can get in the way of learning is to understand that although change we choose for ourselves is often stimulating and energising, it can be very hard for human beings to cope with imposed, endless and inappropriate change. Roger Harrison discovered high levels of exhaustion and burn out amongst public sector participants in his workshops in Australia and New Zealand - people who, like teachers, were suffering from seemingly endless "mandated change" with little room for manoeuvre:

> "Their organisations were in retreat, their clients and colleagues were in shock, and they were feeling inadequate as they tried to drum up enthusiasm for upbeat, forward looking programmes in organisations reeling from one imposed change after another. My discussions with the participants convinced me that it was time to reframe the work of organisational development, making a shift from the idea that organisations needed *agents of change* to the idea that they needed *facilitators of healing*." (Harrison, 1995a: p 166)

The transition curve identified by Adams, Hayes and Hopson (1977), which is derived from understanding the human grieving process, can be very helpful in helping individuals work through painful situations.

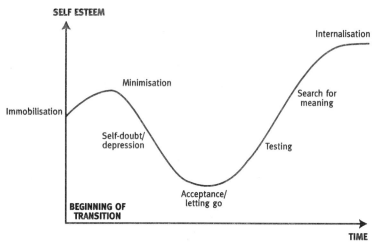

Figure 5.2 The transition curve

A common reaction to an unwanted change is to feel shocked and immobilised. This is often swiftly followed by a period of minimisation and denial. "This can't be allowed to happen, we will resist it, get X on our side." If the resistance is not successful it is possible to slide into a deep trough of self-doubt and depression in which one stays until it becomes possible to accept what has happened and to begin to look forward to an alternative future. The climb out of despond then begins; as new possibilities are tested out, new meaning is made of what has happened and gradually self-esteem is restored or even enhanced by the thought that one has survived a difficult time and grown through it.

Of course, this process is not always smooth. It is easy to lapse back into depression or denial if there are further set backs or when one unwanted happening is followed swiftly by another. Sometimes actions taken in the period of denial can come back to haunt us. In one example, when an LEA determined to amalgamate some neighbouring infant and junior schools into through-primaries to reduce costs, staff in an infant school vigorously campaigned against this. They enlisted the support of parents by explaining their belief that the interests of young children were seldom a priority in through-schools, where attention tended to focus on the needs of older children. They lost the fight and were both shocked and surprised to find that some parents had taken this thought so much to heart that they took their children away from the amalgamated school to send them to another school which had retained its infant status.

Awareness of the transition curve can be helpful during a difficult but inevitable change. Some ways of behaving are definitely more helpful than others. Any element of secrecy and denial of real intent by those initiating the change is likely to increase the steepness of the curve and to lock individuals into anger and denial. Other behaviours can also be very unhelpful. A secondary teacher reported his anger and frustration at his head's statement that "this hurts me more than it hurts you" when breaking the bad news of his redundancy, "The idea that, rather than coping with my own feelings of rejection and the unfairness of it all, I should be feeling sorry for him was the last straw!"

The emergence from self-doubt is a particularly crucial time. Some individuals are more resilient than others and all of us are more or less resilient at different times in our lives. Those most resistant to letting go may try to hold others back with them. Those with more opportunity to move on may deliberately or inadvertently add to the depression of the less fortunate. Small successful steps of any kind can be energising as can the sense of being able to learn something from the experience.

Barriers to change

Per Dalin suggests that there are four main barriers to accepting a change (1978: p.25). The first of these are *value barriers*. These are the barriers created when there are ideological differences between the individuals and groups involved in a change. Different belief systems lead the situation to be perceived from different perspectives. Many teachers come into teaching on the basis of their personal belief and values. They may be attracted to certain types of school, for example, selective or comprehensive, because this reflects their view of the opportunities that should be offered to pupils. Their response to attempts to make changes to the system is likely to be strongly influenced by the match or contradiction with their personal value system.

The second are *power barriers*. Many changes lead to a redistribution of power, and individuals' or groups' attitudes towards change will be influenced by whether they perceive themselves to be increasing or losing their power. The power shift factor was clearly visible in the UK educational reforms of the 1980s and 1990s. Central government, head teachers and school governors gained power at the expense of LEAs and, some would argue, individual teachers whose link with their LEA was weakened or in some cases removed against their preference. As one teacher put it:

> "It's interesting, but since our school was released
> from the oppression of the LEA our head seems to
> have developed some quite effective oppressive
> practices of his own."

Third are the *practical barriers*. Some changes are ill-advised, inappropriate or badly mishandled. In these circumstances resistance may be the natural or the sound response. Dismissing all reservations as merely "resistance to change" is not a stance that enhances organisational learning. Healthy questioning is essential and lack of resistance can lead to ill-thought-out developments being pushed through. Sometimes there has been so much rapid change that individuals start to believe that they have become immune. A group of middle managers in an FE college that had been through an horrendous round of cutbacks, redundancies, pressure for early retirements, job changes, and further cutbacks were quite scornful about the notion that they might find change difficult, "We don't have any problem. We used to make a fuss but it never did any good. We wouldn't dream of resisting change. We just get on with it - whatever it is."

This may have saved them some grief in the short run. However, it is unlikely that people who have learned to shut down their natural resistance and keep their heads down will manage to retain the questioning, creativity and enthusiasm that good teaching needs.

The last of Dalin's barriers is *psychological*. Sometimes an individual or possibly a group may decide that, for whatever personal reason, they simply cannot or will not make this change.

They may have had enough, or problems in the rest of their life may be getting in the way. They may actively dislike the person or people promoting the change and be unwilling to support them. Many teachers and heads left their positions precipitously when their pension arrangements were changed in 1997. Some said that they had meant to work for longer but that they simply could not face the thought of another six or eight years.

Perhaps you can think of a change you have resisted during your career. Which of these barriers do you think was (or were) the most significant? When asked this question, people generally feel more comfortable or even quite proud to have resisted changes because they were against their principles or ill-conceived. Acknowledging power or personal barriers is often more difficult but these are often at least a part of what makes a change hard to accept.

The problem of commitment

It is difficult to ensure engagement or commitment - particularly towards a change that is imposed. Fullan goes so far as to say, "You can't mandate what matters" (1993, p 21) and it is almost certainly true that, on the whole, the higher the commitment the greater the potential for learning. In discussing the power of *Shared Vision*, Senge describes seven possible levels of commitment:

- *Commitment*   - you take action to create what is needed to make it happen.

- *Enrolment*   - you want it to happen.

- *Genuine compliance*   - you agree and do what is expected and needed.

- *Formal compliance*   - you agree on the whole and go along with it.

- *Grudging compliance*   - you don't see the benefits but don't want to get into trouble.

- *Non-compliance*   - you don't see the benefits and won't do it.

- *Apathy*   - you are not interested and have no energy.

Consider in Activity 5.3 whether you can apply these categories of attitude to responses to a change in your school.

Activity 5.3	The problem of commitment

Can you place yourself and your colleagues on this chart in relation to a current change?

	Self	Colleagues
Commitment		
Enrolment		
Genuine compliance		
Formal compliance		
Grudging compliance		
Non-compliance		
Apathy		

Where is the overall balance - towards positive or negative attitudes?

Which are the attitudes that are hardest to spot?

How possible is it for people to acknowledge where they stand in relation to any initiative?

What would help to increase commitment?

What will have to change to make this possible?

(Based on Senge, 1990)

The problem of too much agreement

The last commonly found inhibitor of learning is that of too strong a preference for agreement and consensus. Harvey (1974) tells the story of the *Abilene Paradox* in which he describes a family that is sitting around on a hot and languid Texan afternoon. The father-in-law suggests that they might all like to go to Abilene and one by one everyone agrees. They consequently endure a long, hot, cramped journey in a car without air conditioning and an indifferent meal. On the equally unpleasant journey home the family is horrified to find out that no one had wanted to go to Abilene in the first place, including the person who had made the suggestion. He had been concerned that the others might be bored but he would actually have preferred to stay home and play dominoes. The point was that no one had wanted to seem negative and no one had an alternative to offer.

This situation is mirrored in many work situations. It is great to find yourself working with like-minded people and not to have to battle against others all the time. But this can slip into the Abilene Paradox quite easily. No one wants to be the one who disagrees, so that whatever is suggested is in danger of becoming reality. Ideas are not shaken up, reshaped or fine tuned. Opportunities for learning are reduced. As in Senge's learning disabilities, the frog may be brought gently to the boil.

Placing a high value on collaboration can make dealing positively with difference and conflict seem more difficult. However, it is not conflict itself that is the problem but the failure to handle and use it. Johnson (1990) lists nine potentially constructive outcomes of conflict. It can:

- Make us more aware of problems that need attention

- Encourage change

- Energise

- Make life more interesting

- Lead to better decisions

- Reduce day-to-day irritations (the release of a 'good' argument)

- Help us to understand ourselves better

- Be fun if not taken too seriously

- Enrich relationships longer term.

Johnson proposes five different ways of responding to conflict: withdrawing, forcing, smoothing, compromising and confronting. The first four of these lead us either to suppress or deny our feelings or to impose them on others. Confronting behaviour places value on, and pays attention to, both individual goals and purposes, and the relationship between people. It can result in truly constructive outcomes, with relationships strengthened and all parties satisfied with the outcome and thus more able to resolve future differences.

Working with the organisational shadow

Most of the inhibitors to learning in this chapter are to be found in the hidden or shadow side of organisations where things are often not what they seem. There are many different words to describe the hidden side of people and organisations - informal, dark, hidden, shadow, underside, demonic or doppelganger. Along with the balancing light side, this is a very old idea, found in myth, history and religion. Acknowledgement of the dark side is almost entirely absent from the generally cheerful literature of business and management. Yet we all have a deep sense of the "shadow" and use it in our everyday understanding of the world. When things do go wrong, it is often a sort of negative reflection of what we really wanted to go right. Perhaps the most famous case in myth is that of Faust who sold his soul to the Devil for earthly power and success, but there are plenty of modern examples. There are two ways of thinking about this aspect of organisations.

The informal or hidden aspect

Roger Plant uses the metaphor of an iceberg to differentiate between the formal and informal faces of the organisation. The top of the iceberg, the clearly visible tenth comprises the formal structure, policies, rules and job descriptions but hidden underneath are all the emotions, relationships, values and beliefs, cultures and subcultures that make things so much less straightforward than they seem.

The demonic or double aspect

The negative or evil side which is often an exaggeration, distortion or degeneration of good or positive qualities: hard working becomes workaholism, busyness becomes hyperactivity, concern for others becomes interference, orderliness becomes rigid control. There is a strong potential for the demonic in the current pressure for schools to set themselves targets, preferably those that are SMART: specific, measurable, achievable, realistic and timed. There is a crucial difference between an indicator, which may help to give you an idea of how you are getting on, and a target that directs you to a specific end. The demonic aspect of this is demonstrated, for example, in the emerging trend for schools in the examination league tables to show an improvement in the number of pupils gaining grades A - C in GCSE with no improvement for those with lower grades. Pursuing a target so easily distorts the situation, as it becomes the key focus of energy, often producing results quite contrary to those initially intended.

Change strategies often concentrate on the easily visible formal side of the organisation. As a consequence change programmes and "restructuring" often have little impact once the first stress and inconvenience for some - and excitement for others - is over. This approach assumes that it is possible to separate the rational and the emotional; but anyone who has been involved in an apparently rational reorganisation will know that logic and emotion are more closely intertwined than this. A learning organisation will know better. There will be a general recognition that organisational life is complex, that there are factors that hinder as well as enhance learning, that people's feelings are important and need to be taken into account, that restructuring changes little on its own, and that unless the factors that so easily impede learning are taken seriously and dealt with in some way, comparatively little may be achieved. Now consider the questions in Activity 5.4.

Activity 5.4	**Working with the Shadow**

Think about a recent, planned, reasonably large-scale development in your school

What happened within the formal structure to ensure that this development took place?

What happened in the shadows?

Were there any aspects of the demonic involved?

How did each of the elements effect outcomes for better or worse?

What are the implications for future learning and development in your school?

Leadership in the Learning School

Finally, we come to the issue of leading the learning school. The question for this chapter is about the kind of leadership that is needed: what sort of leading most promotes learning in individuals and organisations? The chapter opens with an exploration of some of the key ideas about leadership that are in circulation, looking both in the light and in the shadow. It then moves to the issue of leading the learning school, and explores the different ways in which leadership itself can be learned. Finally the chapter draws some conclusions about the purpose and role of leadership in the development of a learning school.

What is leadership?

Much is claimed for leadership within the management literature. In the context of education, for example:

- Mortimore *et al* (1988) identify purposeful leadership of staff by the head as a key factor in school effectiveness.

- The National Commission on Education (1993) found strong, positive leadership by the head and senior staff to be a significant feature of successful schools.

- Beare, Caldwell and Milligan go so far as to claim that:

> "Outstanding leadership has invariably emerged as a key characteristic of outstanding schools."(Beare *et al* 1992: p141)

- The TTA *National Standards for Headteachers* (1997: p1) opens its section on the Core Purpose of Headship with the words, "To provide professional leadership for a school which secures its success and improvement".

Much of the research and writing about leadership, both within and outside the field of education, concentrates on the person or persons deemed to be at the top of an organisation. Successful leaders have been identified, interviewed and observed, and generalised conclusions formulated about what leaders are and what they do. It is important to clarify at the outset that there is a crucial difference between *leadership* which can be found and manifested by anyone in any part of an organisation, and being *the leader*, a role that is confined to the person at the top (in the case of schools, the head teacher). Although those at the top of any organisation are required to manifest leadership if they try to corner this activity everyone usually suffers. As Gerard Egan puts it when he is talking about this subject, "If your organisation has only one leader then it is almost certainly short of leadership."

Despite the apparent preoccupation with those at the top, there is increasing agreement that leadership needs to be developed at all levels and within all aspects of schooling. A learning organisation will value leadership wherever it is needed. However, the approach and behaviour of the head teacher is highly significant. Even in the most democratic of schools, the staff looks to the head for signals about which behaviour will be valued and rewarded. For example, in a school where the head teacher leaves work as early as possible, staff may stay working late but feel resentful and in some way abandoned. In far more schools, the head is the chief promoter of a long hours culture. Leaving early, even if visibly laden with marking, comes to be seen by everyone (including the early leaver) to denote lack of commitment. Similarly, the head who claims all successes as his or her own, or treats any attempt to take initiative as an act of insubordination, will have a very different effect on the growth of leadership than one who works to foster development and creativity throughout the school. Those who use their position to dominate others disempower those around them and reduce the overall amount of leadership that is available.

Although leadership is a subject that is much researched, written and talked about, its essence remains mysterious. There is no universal description of what leadership actually is and no guaranteed prescription of how one becomes a leader. Bennis and Nanus found 850 different definitions of leadership in the literature leading them to suggest:

> "Leadership is like the abominable snowman, whose footprints are everywhere but who is nowhere to be seen." (Bennis and Nanus, 1997: p19)

They found it hard to generalise about the 90 successful public and private sector leaders they studied:

> "There seemed to be no obvious pattern for their success. They were right brained, left brained, tall and short, fat and thin, articulate and inarticulate, assertive and retiring, dressed for success and dressed for failure, participative and autocratic. There were more variations than themes. Even their managerial styles were restlessly different." (Bennis and Nanus, 1997: p 24)

This lack of certainty is not reflected in the Teacher Training Agencies' *National Standards for Headteachers* (1997) which is pretty unequivocal about the core purposes, key outcomes, professional knowledge and understanding, skills and attributes and key areas of headship. Not only are these factors clear to the writers of the document they are also seen to be applicable to all aspiring and serving headteachers in all types and sizes of schools.

Your personal perspective on leadership

Leadership is such a commonplace notion that almost everyone has an opinion about it and will be judging those they deem to be leaders against their own particular template. Yet leadership must be a product of human relationships; it cannot be carried out in isolation. If we do not take the time to share and discuss our perceptions and expectations, how can we understand their influence on our behaviour towards each other. The first step is to clarify your own perspective in Activity 6.1.

Activity 6.1	Defining leadership

Think for a moment about your personal view of leadership and then write down a list of 10 words that describe what leadership means to you.

....

....

....

....

....

Now make a list of five people that you would describe as leaders.

1. ....

2. ....

3. ....

4. ....

5. ....

What do they have in common?

What is your definition of leadership?

"Leadership...

Can you match your definition against the five possibilities below:

- Leadership is a matter of *character* - leaders are born not made.

- Leadership derives from *personality* - a person's leadership style will be a reflection of their individual personality.

- Leadership is the *property of groups* - it is about the development of leader/follower relationships.

- Leadership style and behaviour should be appropriate to the *context* - different styles are appropriate in different circumstances.

- Leadership is a function of *culture* - different organisations or groups require and generate different kinds of leadership.

These five views of leadership encapsulate the perspectives most widely found in the writing on leadership and more generally in society.

Some theories of leadership

Reflect for a moment on your own response to four of the ideas in circulation about leadership:

- Blake's Grid

- Contingency Theory

- Transactional Leadership

- Transformational Leadership.

Blake's Grid: The Focus of Leadership

This grid puts together on a matrix two clear dimensions: concern for task and concern for relationships. It refers to management but this grid can clearly equally relate to leadership style.

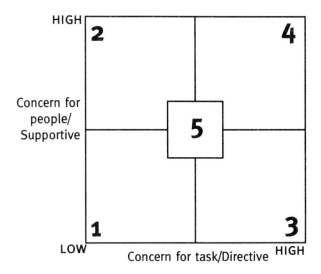

(Based on Blake and Mouton, 1978)

This grid provides five possible positions:

1. *Impoverished Management* where everyone does the absolute minimum to get by.

2. *Country Club Management* where so much attention is paid to the need for satisfying relationships that the task may be neglected.

3. *Authority and Obedience* where the emphasis on completing the task ignores the needs of people.

4. *Team Management* where committed staff work together for common purposes.

5. In the centre is *Organisation/Person Management* where completing the task and maintaining relationships are held in balance.

Contingency Theory

Hersey and Blanchard (1982) provide a similar two-dimensional grid to combine leadership behaviour with follower maturity to produce four leadership decision styles:

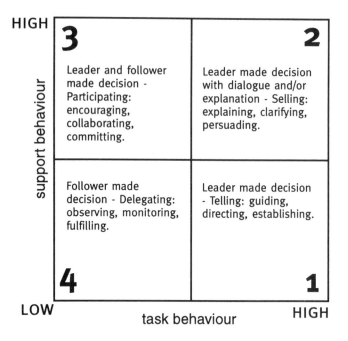

HIGH

support behaviour

3

Leader and follower
made decision -
Participating:
encouraging,
collaborating,
committing.

2

Leader made decision
with dialogue and/or
explanation - Selling:
explaining, clarifying,
persuading.

Follower made
decision - Delegating:
observing, monitoring,
fulfilling.

Leader made decision
- Telling: guiding,
directing, establishing.

4

1

LOW task behaviour HIGH

(Based on Hersey and Blanchard, 1982)

While this can be a useful model and can help us to match leadership style to each different situation, it does have the problem of appearing to assume that leadership and maturity are synonymous. There is clearly potential here for a person in a leadership position to define those around them in a way that suits their personal preference for Telling. How possible do you find it to define the 'maturity' of yourself and your colleagues? How do you think that your colleagues and most particularly your line manager (if you have one) would view you in this context? How much can your level of maturity be attributed to the amount of trust that has been placed in you?

Transactional leadership

This is a matter of clarifying structures, roles, responsibilities and relationships and getting things done on the basis of a straightforward exchange between leaders and followers, "If you do this job well your reward will be ... If not ..." This process can be based on relatively low mutual trust but this is not inevitable. The transactions can embody some important key values, for example, keeping promises, honesty, fairness, trust and regard.

Transformational leadership

Transformational leadership is a qualitatively different approach and is currently being widely promoted as the one most likely to achieve results above the ordinary and to inspire others to great things. There can be much hyperbole here. Such leaders are said to engage their followers' hearts and souls, ensure their commitment to a transforming vision. Transformational leadership should not be confused with charisma: and it is as well to remember that many an inspirational leader has led his or her followers into the abyss. Grace takes this notion beyond the individual in emphasising that:

> "Transformative leadership involves considerable
> social skills of advocacy, intergroup relations, team
> building and inspiration without domination."
> (Grace, 1997: p63)

He proposes that this kind of leadership is exercised by a "community of leaders" as a reflection of the permeation of democratic values which will "transform the nature of leadership itself". Consider these perspectives in Activity 6.2.

Activity 6.2	Theories of Leadership

Consider these different perspectives on leadership and ask yourself which of these styles predominates in your school and/or department?

	A lot like us	A bit like us	Not like us
Focus on task	☐	☐	☐
Focus on relationship	☐	☐	☐
Contingency theory	☐	☐	☐
Transactional leadership	☐	☐	☐
Transformational leadership	☐	☐	☐

How does each relate to your own favoured leadership style?

	A lot like me	A bit like me	Not like me
Focus on task	☐	☐	☐
Focus on relationship	☐	☐	☐
Contingency theory	☐	☐	☐
Transactional leadership	☐	☐	☐
Transformational leadership	☐	☐	☐

Your personal belief or theory about what leadership is will almost certainly influence both your own behaviour and your reactions to the way that people behave towards you. For example, a group of teachers on an INSET day were engaged in a series of problem solving activities. One person was absolutely dominant, making suggestions, organising the group, making her voice heard. In the debriefing session it became clear that, although everyone else had understood the exercise to be about team work, this person had assumed that it was about demonstrating leadership and that, for her, leadership was about being in charge.

The behaviours and characteristics of leaders

What conclusions can be drawn from the rapidly proliferating studies of leadership? The two following examples encompass much of what is emerging. Kouzes and Posner (1987) focus on the behaviour of leaders. They look at what 'successful' leaders do. You may find it helpful to consider your reactions to their Five Practices and Ten Commitments which are as follows.

Challenging the process

• *Search for opportunities and experiment and take risks*

Leaders are pioneers but this does not mean that they themselves must produce all the ideas. The skill lies in recognising, supporting and encouraging new ideas and in being willing to challenge the system itself if it is inhibiting development.

Inspiring a shared vision

• *Envision the future and enlist others*

Leadership is not about pursuing a solitary vision, like the poet John Clare who set off from home alone to find the horizon when he was three years old. The vision or purpose must be shared.

Enabling others to act

• *Foster collaboration and strengthen others*

Leadership is not about solitary success. It is about sharing the task and involving others. This practise is at the heart of one of the oldest and most often quoted descriptions of leadership:

> "As for the best leaders, the people do not notice their
> existence; the next best, the people honour and praise;
> the next the people fear and the next the people hate.
> But when the best leader's work is done, the people
> say we did it ourselves." (Lao Tse)

Modelling the way

• *Set the example and plan small wins*

We must practice what we preach. Any vision will soon fade if it becomes clear that the person apparently espousing it lacks personal commitment. It is also important to experience early success, because as we adjust to a new way of doing things we find that matters often get worse before they get better. This leads to the final practice.

Encouraging the heart

• *Recognise individual contribution and celebrate accomplishments*

The focus here is on the importance of encouragement. Some of the examples that Kouzes and Posner offer in this context - of stickers, T-shirts and badges (for adults) - may ring rather oddly in non-American ears, but not the principle that praise and celebration are essential and often underrated activities.

How would leadership in your school match up to these aspirations?

Despite their initial difficulties, Bennis and Nanus have reached some conclusions about the nature of leadership. They emphasise that:

- Leadership is about character. The kind of person you are will influence the kind of leader you can be. They describe the process of becoming a leader as being much the same as that of becoming an integrated human being.

- Leaders must be social architects. Organisations require more than formal structures, and it is necessary to design organisations in a way that promotes innovation, imagination, creativity and creates intellectual capital.

- Leaders must have a strong determination to achieve a goal or realise a vision.

- A central capacity for leaders is that of generating and sustaining trust. This is the glue that holds things together. It is very hard to gain, and alarmingly easy to lose.

- Leaders have an inclination to engage in action that results in success, a capacity to turn vision into reality. (Bennis and Nanus, 1997: ppix-xiv)

Manifesting leadership

Leadership has many different facets and can occur in almost any context. Anyone can manifest leadership of some kind unless they are prevented in some way from doing so. Sometimes the inhibition is from a dominant other but at other times, especially if we lack formal status, it comes from within us because:

> "To assert one's leadership as a teacher ... takes commitment to an educational ideal. It also requires the energy to overcome one's own inertia caused by habit and overwork. And it requires a certain kind of courage to step outside of the small prescribed circle of the traditional 'teacher tasks', to declare through our actions that we care about and take responsibility for more than the minimum, more than what goes on within the four walls of our classroom." (Barth 1990: p131).

Activity 6.3 is an opportunity to reflect on leadership qualities.

Activity 6.3	**Manifesting leadership**

Think about a time recently when your have displayed leadership qualities at work:

What did you do?

Who else was involved?

Which factors ensured your commitment, energy and courage?

What have you learned about yourself and about acts of leadership?

Sometimes understanding what we do *not* regard as leadership can be equally helpful. A teacher describing his new head said:

"He is very pleasant, very personable, very easy to talk to. It really feels as though he listens. But in a way that's the problem. He's like that with everyone;

he agrees with everyone. That means one week he's
very enthusiastic with one thing and the next week
it's something quite different. It's as though there's no
core. It's impossible to know what he stands for."

After listening to a senior LEA officer explaining the steps that
would have to be taken in the light of cuts in funding, another
teacher commented:

"I know she's very able. I believe she'll have found
the best possible solution. I trust her judgement but I
wish that I felt that she cares about what she's having
to do."

These teachers are expressing their perceptions of what leadership
might be by noting its absence. Contact with these people in key
leadership positions has not filled them with commitment, energy
and courage.

The dilemmas of leadership

There are many dilemmas inherent in the leadership role. Some of
these are generated by the more general contradictions in the
expectations that are placed upon individuals and organisations.
Rosabeth Moss Kanter provides a salutary list of some of these:

- *"Think strategically and invest in the future* - but keep
  the numbers up today.

- *Be entrepreneurial and take risks* - but don't cost the
  business anything by failing.

- *Continue to do everything you're currently doing even
  better* - and spend more time communicating with
  employees, serving on teams, and launching new
  projects.

- *Know every detail of your business* - but delegate more responsibility to others.

- *Become passionately dedicated to 'visions' and fanatically committed to carrying them out* - but be flexible, responsive, and able to change direction quickly.

- *Speak up, be a leader, set the direction* - but be participative, listen well, co-operate.

- *Throw yourself wholeheartedly into the entrepreneurial game and the long hours it takes* - and stay fit.

- *Succeed, succeed, succeed* - and raise terrific children." (Kanter, 1989: pp 20-21)

Leadership is fraught with such dichotomies. How does one take the lead without disenfranchising others? How can one be inspirational when dealing with a colleague who is not pulling his or her weight? And how does one manage the dilemmas inherent in the three core issues of:

- Creating a vision

- Using power

- Living with the shadow side of leadership.

Creating a vision

The issue of creating and inspiring vision is central to much of current thinking on leadership. In addition to the many references to creating a vision throughout this book, it is the first of the leadership skills identified by the TTA in their "Skills and Attributes" of headship:

"Headteachers should be able to:
i) create and secure commitment to a clear vision
for an effective institution." (TTA, 1997: p.4).

There have been many references in this book about the power of shared vision. The notion of the learning school is itself a vision, an aspiration to aim for. However, the briefest glimpse of human history will be redolent with warnings that the human propensity for following visionary leaders is fraught with peril. Some of the writing on successful leaders does not seem to question the nature of their visions. The key criterion seems to be organisational success without questioning the nature of the fundamental purpose. Vision per se will not do, particularly in the context of the education of children. Hodgkinson (1991) is clear that educational leadership is a moral art and describes:

> "The unending duty of the moral leader - the conscious struggle to blend action with thoughtful consideration of values and moral responsibilities in taking decisions."

The vision for your school must be appropriate to, and congruent with, its fundamental purpose. It must be directed towards an attractive but realistic future. Vision and values must be connected although this may not be easy, as some desirable values can be hard to reconcile. How does a school aim to promote both excellence and equity in the current climate, for example? A vision must have meaning for all concerned. Headteachers with compelling personal visions that are not widely shared by their staff, governors or parents are likely to produce bitterly divided schools, however noble their intent. As Sergiovanni explains:

> "Leadership reality for all groups is the reality they create for themselves, and thus leadership cannot exist separate from what people find significant and meaningful."(Sergiovanni, 1987: p116)

Using power

It is not possible to ignore the issue of power when discussing leadership. Attitudes to, and beliefs about, power have considerable impact on leadership behaviour. An issue which is absolutely central is whether you believe that power in any situation or organisation is finite (the zero sum game). The view leads those who feel they have power to be defensive and those without power to see the only solution as being to seize and redistribute it. If, however, you believe that power is infinite, that the more it is shared the more there will be, you will be more willing and able to share it with others. There is also a fundamental difference between seeking power over others and seeing power as being created with and through them.

There are different kinds of power:

- *Coercive power*   depending on threat and punishment

- *Personal power*   persuasiveness, charisma

- *Expert power*   derived from specialist knowledge that others do not possess

- *Role power*   derived from position or status

- *Reward power*   being able to reward others financially or through promotion

- *Connection power*   derived from networks and relationships.

With the exception of the first, all of these can all be used positively although none seems to be automatically connected to learning. Indeed, the unscrupulous pursuance of any of these might very well get in the way of it.

Activity 6.4 — Your power inventory

First consider which sources of power you have access to in your organisation?

	A lot	Some	Little or none
Coercive power	☐	☐	☐
Personal power	☐	☐	☐
Expert power	☐	☐	☐
Role power	☐	☐	☐
Reward power	☐	☐	☐
Connection power	☐	☐	☐
Other	☐	☐	☐

Now reflect on what you do with your power. Do you use it:
- to get things done
- to enhance your own position
- to enhance others
- to enhance learning?

What do you want to use more or less of and why?

Living with the shadow side of leadership

The downside of leadership has been alluded to at various points in this chapter. The leadership shadow has many facets. There is the problem of leaders who abuse their legitimate sources of power in one way or another: there are those who use their seniority, their personal or even physical power to bully or seduce; those who own and control their expertise in a way that excludes and diminishes colleagues; those who use their status to block others' initiative or to lay claim to their successes; those who use their control over the reward systems to manipulate, patronise and punish; those use their networks to discredit others.

There is, however, another aspect to this. Those in leadership positions can be manipulated by others into particular forms of behaviour. For example, I visited a head teacher who was describing to me the difficulty she had in persuading the staff in her new school to make decisions for themselves. At that moment there was a knock on the door. It was a teacher wanting to know if she could provide some school gym shoes for a child who had come to school with soaking wet shoes and had no others of his own. "Of course you can," said the head, "you don't need to ask me first." The teacher looked furious. "We have always had to ask before," she replied in a manner that made it quite clear that she had little respect for a head who was prepared to allow such licence.

George Orwell describes how he found himself as a young man in Burma with great reluctance having to shoot an elephant that was rampaging through the bazaar. As a police officer with a gun he was expected to deal with this problem, and an immense crowd came along to see that he did:

> "And suddenly I realised that I should have to shoot the
> elephant after all. The people expected it of me and I
> had got to do it; I could feel their two thousand wills
> pressing me forward irresistibly." (Orwell, 1957: p95)

Rather than be the leading actor in this piece as he appeared, Orwell found he was in fact an "absurd puppet pushed to and fro" by the will of the crowd (Orwell, 1957, p95).

This tendency of individuals or groups to require others to take responsibility for them was explored by Bion during the Second World War and afterwards in the Tavistock Institute. He identifies three basic assumptions to be found in groups:

1. *Dependency* - a group manifesting this assumption will want their leader to look after, protect them and keep them feeling good. The leader might have left or even have died, in which case the group will protect themselves from unpleasantness by deciding what their leader would have said or thought rather than facing up to the difficulty themselves.

2. *Fight-flight* - here the group is preoccupied with defence against some kind of enemy. They look to the leader to devise some action, a plan that they can follow. This provides a sense of togetherness, but again absolves individuals from taking responsibility.

3. *Pairing* - here the group concentrates on getting on well together and hoping that somehow the future will be better. The leader's job is to confirm this belief without actually doing anything to disturb things or to make any changes in practice.

The shadow is of course always with us, but it is important to recognise that many elements of the current pressures on schools contain elements that are likely to enhance its demonic aspects. For example, the current emphasis on specific aspects of performance, target setting, assessment, inspection, the general climate which endorses naming and shaming, these all tend to increase the desire to take control, to displace the blame or to be absolved from responsibility, all of which will minimise learning.

Leading the learning school

Senge makes a strong link between leaders and learning:

> "In a learning organisation they are designers, stewards
> and teachers. They are responsible for building
> organisations where people continually expand their
> capabilities to understand complexity, clarify vision, and
> improve shared mental models - that is, they are
> responsible for learning." (Senge, 1990: p340)

But it seems clear that a learning school will not require a hero/ine leader; a headteacher who single-handedly sets the direction, makes all the important decisions and then ensures that others commit themselves to these. Fullan and Hargreaves (1992) neatly sum up the factors that enhance leadership in collaborative and learning schools. They see the development of widespread leadership as being dependent on:

- The action of the heads in those schools

- The kind of leadership, not charismatic, innovative, high flying but a more subtle kind that makes activity meaningful for others

- Leadership coming from a variety of sources in the school.

A headteacher has a critical role to play but should not corner all the leadership activity for him or herself. Equally, others in the school should not abdicate their responsibility for taking the lead when necessary and appropriate. Leadership can also be seen "as a quality of organisations - a systematic characteristic" (Ogawa and Bossert, 1995). From this perspective it is possible to perceive leadership as a source of energy pervading all aspects of school life which can be tracked and mapped throughout. For example, if we return to the Energy Flow Model from Chapter 4, we can see opportunities to exercise leadership at all four of the key interfaces.

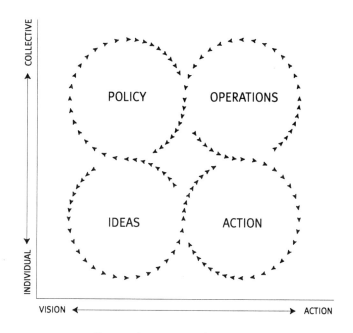

Figure 6.1 Energy Flow Model

The interface between policy and operations is where leadership is needed to transform policy into joint action. Policy aspirations need to be translated into workable practice. Someone must lead this process and work with colleagues to develop processes, systems and structures to ensure that this happens. Curriculum leadership will be needed at the interface between operations and individual action. Individual learning, found at the interface between individual ideas and action, needs to be shared and made public in an atmosphere of openness and genuine enquiry. Individuals who have been engaged in putting shared decisions into practice in their classrooms need to report back on what they have learned and why. The interface between individual ideas and policy making is where the outcomes of the policy are fed back and reflected upon thus enhancing the process of policy development. It is where the consequences of the shared vision are made plain. Leadership may be particularly important in this context as this is the area that most organisations seem to find most difficult. This is where we must all stop grumbling about the system and take systemic action to change things.

Chapter 1 identified the four fundamental characteristics of a learning school. These were:

- A commitment to lifelong learning for all those within a school

- An emphasis on collaborative learning and the creative use of difference and conflict

- A holistic understanding of the school as a whole organisation

- Strong connections and relationships with the community and the world outside the school.

These characteristics are equally relevant to the issue of individual leadership. They suggest that those manifesting leadership in a learning school will need to:

- Be open to (although not uncritical of) new ideas and visibly engage in personal and professional learning

- Recognise, acknowledge and value the same approach in others

- Value difference and be able to confront conflict creatively

- Think at the level of the whole organisation even when engaged in their day-to-day activities

- Keep in active touch with the wider world outside the school.

They will both share and influence the school's vision or purpose and this will inform their individual practice. They will be willing to learn from colleagues, pupils and the wider community. A further crucial ability is what Alan Langlands describes as the "power of synthesis". He describes leaders in the NHS who are able to absorb the complex policies that "rain down from the centre", the variety of activities and pressures within their organisations, the needs and demands of their communities and somehow make sense of it all. (1996: p24) Such sense-making ability is also needed in education.

Above all, those manifesting leadership in a learning school must be prepared to grapple with the contentious issues that face schools. They will not set aside:

> "the human and the humane ... passion and conviction...The difficult and divisive questions, the questions of purpose and morality, the questions arising from the necessary impositions of one person's will upon another, the questions that challenge the linking of ends and means ... in the search for a pallid consensus and an illusory effectiveness" (Greenfield and Ribbens, 1993: p165-5)

Learning to lead

Much of the writing about leadership is concerned with what leaders do rather than how people become leaders. Yet:

> "The belief that leadership cannot be learned is a far more powerful deterrent to development than is the nature of the leadership process itself." (Kouzes and Posner, 1987)

Learning about, and learning to share, leadership will be valued activities in a learning school. Individuals will need the opportunity to access such learning but will also have to exercise some personal responsibility and self direction. Here are seven possible ways to enhance such learning:

- Taking the opportunity to lead
- Taking the opportunity to acquire experience outside one's normal role
- Formal learning

- Mentoring

- Learning from role models

- Learning with others

- Learning in the organisational context

- Learning from leading.

As you read the following explanations, consider which of them might be a helpful next step for you and, if you are well supplied with opportunities for learning about leadership, which you will try to make more available to others.

Opportunity to take the lead in an organisational project
There are many opportunities to take on leadership roles in schools. The role of curriculum co-ordinator has obvious potential in primary schools and there are many others within secondary schools. The choice of the word co-ordinator for many of these tasks is interesting. It may be a reflection of the desire to be collaborative but, alternatively, it may demonstrate the misunderstanding that only those at the top of the hierarchy can lead. Perhaps the notion of leadership could be reclaimed in these contexts. How are developments that need to be led shared in your school? How tight a hold do senior staff keep? Are individuals allowed to take initiative and risk failure, or is the emphasis on co-ordination and consensus at the expense of creativity?

Opportunity for experience outside one's normal role
It can be difficult for teachers daily engaged in their classrooms to have opportunities to widen their horizons. Collaboration between departments/year groups or between schools or within local or national bodies can offer this chance provided it is not resented by colleagues but valued as a legitimate activity. Is such activity valued in your school?

Mentoring
Mentoring for new and existing headteachers is becoming

widespread and many other teachers attribute some aspects of their development to a colleague who has offered them the support and challenge inherent in a good mentoring relationship at moments in their career. However, most of these relationships seem to be a matter of chance rather than design. Do you have anyone who fulfils this role at the moment? Are you offering it to anyone else? If not what steps might you take to change this situation?

Formal learning

Some people learn about leadership from attending courses or taking a higher degree. In the future all applicants for headship in the UK will have to undertake a national qualification embodying standards and consistency and which refers throughout its documentation to training rather than learning. There is clearly great potential here but there is also a fear that this could lead to an unhealthy degree of conformity. The story of Procrustes is salutary in this context. He claimed that his bed was exactly the right size for all his visitors and either amputated any extraneous bits or had his visitors stretched to ensure that they would fit. It is also possible to be interested in leadership but not in headship. Where do you look for external challenge, stimulation and formal learning?

Learning from role models

Much learning about leadership comes from watching others in action. Both good and bad examples can be helpful but it is necessary to do more than imitate or reject. Leadership is a complex and multi-faceted skill in which the people involved, the wider context, the specific task, the previous history and future aspirations are all interwoven. Others' experiences are not easily transferable but may help us to increase our options and our understanding. What are you learning, from whom and why?

Learning with others

Action learning sets as described in Chapter 2, or any other kind of support group or learning partnership where you will have to reflect on and articulate your experience will be almost certain to enhance your ability to learn about leadership.

Learning in an organisational context

This kind of learning requires us to consciously learn from our organisational context. Many of the activities in this book have been designed to help you to do this. Bennis and Nanus say that leaders:

> "... are able to concentrate on what matters most to the organization and to use the organization as a learning environment ... (to become) the leader in organizational learning, the management of the collective self." (Bennis and Nanus, 1997: pp116-17)

Learning from leading

Much crucial learning has to take place in the heat of the action. Like parenting and many other human activities, even the most rigorous reflection and preparation will have its limitations. The most difficult situation is likely to be when you have to do this learning in the exposed position of being appointed leader. In any senior position, and most particularly as a new head, it may be difficult if not impossible to acknowledge any vulnerability, especially if there are those around you who applied unsuccessfully for the job. It is not that you should run around asking others what you should do, but it may be possible to acknowledge that you are on a learning curve and that you do not always get it right first time. If you try to separate yourself from your colleagues and be *the* leader any problems will almost certainly be exacerbated. If you declare your task to be that of developing creative leadership and learning throughout the school, you will have a very different starting point and both you and your school will have a greatly enhanced potential.

Leading organisational learning

Activity 6.5 asks you to connect leadership and organisational learning in you school and to begin to map this process.

Activity 6.5 — Leadership and organisational learning

Start by listing five areas of developmental activity in your school. Who is taking a leadership role in these areas? What is the organisation learning from these processes?

	Activity	Leadership	Organisational learning
1.			
2.			
3.			
4.			
5.			

How sound is the connection between leadership and learning?

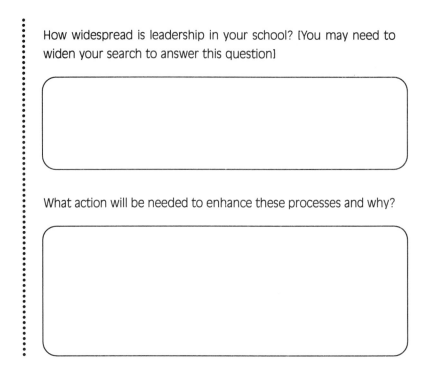

How widespread is leadership in your school? [You may need to widen your search to answer this question]

What action will be needed to enhance these processes and why?

Leadership is a fundamental ingredient in developing a learning organisation. It is required at all levels, to embody the sense of purpose and direction, to develop the five disciplines, to enhance the energy flow, to seek out learning opportunities, to take risks, to be persistent, and to keep up courage. It is a subtle, synthesising source of energy flowing between all those within the school and its community. The more that leadership is shared, the more of it there will be and the more it will be possible for the school and its pupils to achieve.

The last image in this book is borrowed from Dr Angela Arien and the work of the naturalist Milton Olton (see Fritchie, 1996: pp 62-63). It likens the nature of leadership in the learning school to that of a skein of geese in flight. As each bird flaps its wings it creates an uplift for the bird behind. By flying in a V formation, the flock has a 71 per cent greater flying range than if each bird flew alone. When a goose falls out of the skein, and finds how strong is the drag outside, it resumes its place as quickly as it can. When the lead goose feels tired it drops back a little, another takes its place and the skein flies on. If a goose becomes ill or injured and falls out of the formation, two other geese leave with it and stay until it recovers or dies. They then rejoin their flock or find another. The noise you hear as the skein sweeps overhead is a message of support from the geese temporarily at the back of the skein. They are honking their encouragement to those that are ahead.

SOURCES

Adams JD, Hayes J and Hopson P (1977) *Transition: Understanding and Managing Personal Change.*

Argyris C and Schon D (1978) *Organisational Learning: A Theory of Action Perspective.* Reading, Mass, Addison-Wesley.

Aspinwall K, Simkins T, Wilkinson J and McAuley J (1992) *Evaluation in Education: A Developmental Approach.* Maidenhead, McGraw-Hill.

Aspinwall K, Garrett V and Owen-Jackson G (1994) "In at the beginning", in Reid I, Constable H and Griffiths R *Teacher Education Reform: The Research Evidence.* London, Chapman.

Baddeley S and James K (1987) "Owl, fox, donkey or sheep: Political skills for managers" *Management Education and Development,* vol 18 part 1, pp 3-19.

Ball S (1994) *Education Reform: A Critical and Post-structuralist Approach.* Buckingham, Open University Press.

Barth R (1990) *Improving Schools from Within: Teachers, Parents and Principals Can Make a Difference.* San Fransisco, Jossey Bass.

Beare H, Caldwell B, Milligan R, (1993) "Leadership", in Preedy, M. (ed) *Managing the Effective School.* London, PCP (in assoc with) The Open University.

Belbin M (1981) *Management Teams.* London, Heineman

Bennis W and Nanus B (1997) *Leaders: Strategies for Taking Charge.* New York, HarperCollins.

Blake R and Mouton J (1978) *The New Managerial Grid.* Maidenhead, McGraw-Hill.

Bottery M (1992) *The Ethics of Education Management.* London, Cassell.

Briggs, Myers I and Myers PB (1990) *Gifts Differing.* Palo Alto, CA, Consulting Psychologists Press.

Canadian Institute of Advanced Research (CIAR) (1992) *The Learning Society.* Toronto, Ontario, CIAR.

Casey D (1993) *Managing Learning in Organizations.* Buckingham, Open University Press.

Coad A (1996) "Smart work and hard work: explicating a learning orientation in strategic management accounting" *Management Accounting Research 7*, pp387-408.

Curriculum in Action (1980) Buckingham, The Open University Press

Dalin P (1978) *Limits to Educational Change.* London and Basingstoke, The McMillan Press.

Egan G (1993) *Adding Value: A Systematic Guide to Business Driven Management and Leadership.* San Francisco, Jossey Bass.

Fritchie R (1996) "Conclusion", in Aspinwall KA (ed) *The First York Symposium on Health.* York, University of York.

Fullan M (1993) *Change Forces: Probing the Depth of Educational Reform.* London, The Falmer Press.

Fullan M and Hargreaves A (1991) *What's Worth Fighting For in Your School?* Buckingham, Open University Press.

Garratt R (1987) *The Learning Organisation.* London, Fontana.

Grace G (1995) "Critical Leadership Studies" in Crawford M, Kydd L and Richards C (eds) *Leadership and Teams in Educational Management.* Buckingham, Open University Press.

Greenfield T and Ribbens P (eds) (1993) *Greenfield on Educational Administration: Towards a Humane Science.* London, Routledge.

Harrison R (1995) A *Consultant's Journey.* Maidenhead, McGraw-Hill.

Harrison R (1995) *Collected Papers of Roger Harrison.* Maidenhead, McGraw-Hill.

Harvey J (1989) *The Abilene Paradox.* San Diego, CA, University Associates.

Hersey P and Blanchard K (1988) *Management of Organizational Behaviour: Utilising Human Resources.* Englewood Cliffs, NJ, Prentice-Hall.

Hodgkinson C (1991) *Educational Leadership: The Moral Art.* Albany, NY, University of New York Press.

Hutton W (1995) *The State We're In.* London, Jonathon Cape.

Johnson D (1990) *Reaching Out: Interpersonal Effectiveness and Self-actualisation.* Englewood Cliffs, NJ, Prentice-Hall.

Jung C G (1971) *Psychological Types.* London, Routledge & Kegan Paul.

Kanter RM (1989) *When Giants Learn to Dance*. London, Simon & Schuster.

Keirsey D and Bates M (1984) *Please Understand Me: Character and Temperament Types*. Del Mar, CA, Prometheus Nemesis.

Kelly GA (1955) *The Psychology of Personal Constructs vols 1 and 2.* London, Routledge.

Kolb D(1971) *Organizational Psychology: An Experiential Approach.* Englewood Cliffs, NJ, Prentice-Hall

Kouzes J and Posner B (1987) *The Leadership Challenge: How to Get Extraordinary Things Done in Organizations.* San Francisco,CA, Jossey Bass.

Langlands A (1996), "A view from here: A personal perspective on the NHS" in Aspinwall KA (ed) *The First York Symposium on Health.* York, University of York.

Little J (1981) "The power of the organisational setting" (paper adapted from final report, *School Success and Staff Development)*.Washington DC, National Institute Of Education.

Louis K and Miles M (1990) *Improving the Urban High School: What Works and Why?* New York, Teachers College Press.

Morgan G (1997) *Images of Organisation.* London, Sage.

Mortimore P et al (1988) *School Matters: The Junior Years.* Somerset, Open Books.

Murdoch I (1992) *Metaphysics as a Guide to Morals.* London, Chatto & Windus.

National Commission on Education (1993). London

Nias J, Southworth G and Yoemans R (1989) *Staff Relationships in the Primary School.* London, Cassell.

Ogawa R and Bossert T (1997) "Leadership as an organisational quality" in Crawford M, Kydd L and Richards C (eds) *Leadership and Teams in Educational Management.* Buckingham, Open University Press.

Orwell G *Inside the Whale and Other Essays.* Harmondsworth, Penguin.

Pascale R(1990) *Managing on the Edge.* Harmondsworth, Penguin.

Pedler M and Aspinwall K (1996) *'Perfect plc?':* The Purpose and Practice of Organisational Learning. Maidenhead, McGraw-Hill.

Pedler M, Burgoyne J and Boydell T (1997) *The Learning Company : A Strategy for Sustainable Development.* Maidenhead, McGraw-Hill (2nd edition).

Pirsig RM (1974) *Zen and the Art of Motorcycle Maintenance.* London, Vintage.

Peters T and Waterman R (1982) *In Search of Excellence.* New York, Harper & Row.

Plant R (1987) *Managing Change and Making It Stick.* London, Fontana.

Pring R (1995) *Closing the Gap: Liberal Education and Vocational Preparation.* London, Hodder & Stoughton.

Reid K, Hopkins D and Holly P(1987) *Towards the Effective School.* Oxford, Blackwell.

Revans R W (1998) *ABC of Action Learning.* London, Lemos & Crane.

Rosenholtz S (1989) *Teachers' Workplace: The Social Organisation of Schools.* New York, Longman.

Sarason S (1990) *The Predictable Failure of Educational Reform.* San Fransisco, Jossey Bass.

Schon D (1971) *Beyond the Stable State.* New York, Random House.

Senge P (1990) *The Fifth Discipline.* New York, Doubleday.

Senge P (1991) "The learning organisation made plain", *Training and Development,* Oct 1991, pp37-64.

Sergiovanni T (1992) *Moral Leadership.* San Fransisco, CA, Jossey Bass.

Sirotnik K (1990) "Society, schooling, teaching and preparing to teach" in Goodland et al (eds) *The Moral Dimensions of Teaching.* San Fransisco, CA, Jossey Bass, pp 296-327.

Stewart R (1982) *Choices for the Manager: a guide to managerial work and behaviour.* London, McGraw-Hill.

TTA (1997) *National Standards for Headteachers.* London, Teacher Training Agency.

INDEX

Action learning, 46-49
Activity
  action learning, 48-49
  assessing school's stage of
    consciousness, 15-16
  characteristics of learning
    company questionnaire, 81-84
  defining leadership, 122-124
  defining your learning
    school, 93-94
  encouraging learning
    in school, 19-21
  energy flow activity, 90-91
  how/why ladder, 76-77
  kind of place, 55-56
  leadership and organisational
    learning, 147-148
  managing blocks to
    learning, 39-40
  manifesting leadership, 131-132
  mental models, 12
  organisational learning styles
    inventory, 58-63
  power inventory, 137
  problem of commitment, 112-113
  reflecting on learning, 31-32
  stakeholder analysis, 74-75
  team roles, 43
  theories of leadership, 127-128
  using metaphorical thinking, 8-9
  valuing difference, 37-38
  view from here, 52-54
  working with shadow, 117
Agreement
  too much agreement, 114-115

Balancing organisational learning
  styles, 69-70

Behaviour of leaders, 129-131
Blake's grid, 124-125
Blocks to learning
  barriers to change, 109-111
  commitment, problem of, 111-113
  generally, 38-39
  learning disabilities in
    organisations, 99-101
  management of, 39-40
  mandated change and innovation
    fatigue, 107-109
  organisational politics, 102-104
  organisational toxicity index, 96-99
  power barriers, 110
  practical barriers, 110
  psychological barriers, 110-111
  time, problem of, 104-106
  too much agreement, 114-115
  value barriers, 109
  working with shadow, 115-117
Boundary workers
  environmental scanners, as, 80
Brains
  organisations as, 7
Budgetary control, 79

Characteristics of learning
  school, 24-25
Climate of learning, 80-81
Collaborative enquiry
  concept of, 23-24
Commitment
  levels of, 111-112
  problem of, 111-113
Concept of learning organisation, 10
Consciousness of organisation
  school's stage of
    consciousness, 15-16

stages of, *14-15*
Contingency theory, *125-126*
Creating learning school
  benefits of learning enriched
    school, *18-19*
  categories of school, *16-18*
  encouraging learning, *19-21*
  kind of learning needed, *22-24*
Creating vision, *134-139*
Critical awareness
  characteristics of, *67-68*
Cultures
  organisations as, *7*

Defining leadership, *122-124*
Defining your learning school, *93-94*
Demoralised teachers, *3-4*
Developing organisational learning
  styles, *69-70*
Dilemmas of leadership, *133-134*
Disciplines of learning organisation
  personal mastery, *10-11*
  shared vision, *13*
  sharing mental models, *11-13*
  summary, *10*
  systems thinking, *14*
  team learning, *13-14*
Dissatisfaction index, *85*

Education
  moral purpose, *5-6*
Enabling others to act, *129*
Enabling structures, *80*
Energy flow model, *85-93*
Enquiry
  characteristics of, *67-68*
Environmental scanners
  boundary workers as, *80*
Excellence
  search for, *5*
Experience outside normal role, *144*

Experiment
  characteristics of, *66-67*

Flux and transformation
  organisations as, *7*
Focus of leadership, *124-125*
Formal learning, *145*
Formative accounting and
  control, *79*

GNVQs
  introduction of, *22*

Habits
  characteristics of, *63-64*
  memory distinguished from, *64-65*
Headteachers
  image of headship, *5*

Image of headship, *5*
Imitation
  characteristics of, *65-66*
Informating
  formative accounting and
    control, *79*
  meaning, *78-79*
Innovation fatigue
  mandated change and, *107-109*
Instruments of domination
  organisations as, *7*
Inter-company learning, *80*
Internal exchange
  value of, *79*
Inventory
  organisational learning
    styles, *58-63*
  power, *137*

Knowledge
  concept of, *22*

Leadership
  behaviour of leaders, *129-131*
  Blake's grid, *124-125*
  challenging process, *129*
  characteristics of, *119-124*
  contingency theory, *125-126*
  creating vision, *134-139*
  defining, *122-124*
  dilemmas of, *133-134*
  enabling others to act, *129*
  encouraging heart, *130-131*
  experience outside one's normal
    role, *144*
  focus of, *124-125*
  formal learning, *145*
  generally, *119*
  inspiring shared vision, *129*
  leading learning school, *140-143*
  leading organisational
    learning, *146-149*
  learning from leading, *146*
  learning to lead, *143-144*
  learning with others, *145*
  living with shadow
    side of, *138-139*
  manifesting, *131-133*
  mentoring, *144-145*
  modelling way, *130*
  organisational context, learning
    in, *146*
  organisational project, taking
    lead in, *144*
  personal perspective on, *122*
  role models, learning from, *145*
  theories of, *124-131*
  transactional, *126-127*
  transformational, *127-129*
  using power, *135-137*
Learning
  action learning, *46-48*
  blocks to, *38-40*
  formal, *145*
  use of term, *4*
  inter-company, *80*
  leading, from, *146*
  learning to lead, *143-144*
  moral requirements, *72*
  nature of, *27-33*
  organisational context, in, *146*
  orientation, *30*
  pupil and teacher, *28-29*
  purpose of, *71-77*
  reflecting on, *31-32*
  role models, from, *145*
  strategy, approach to, *78*
  styles, *33-38*
  supporting groups and
    relationships, *45-46*
  teams, in, *40-49*
  types of, *22-24*
  valuing difference, *37-38*
  with others, *145*
Learning climate, *80-81*
Learning company
  characteristics of
    questionnaire, *81-84*
  inter-company learning, *80*
  use of term, *4*
Learning disabilities, *99-101*
Learning enriched school
  benefits of, *18-19*
  characteristics of, *17-18*
Learning impoverished school
  characteristics of, *17*
Learning organisation
  characteristics of, *77-85*
  concept of, *10*
  consciousness of, *14-16*
  five disciplines for,
    personal mastery, *10-11*
    shared vision, *13*
    sharing mental models, *11-13*

summary, *10*
systems thinking, *14*
team learning, *13-14*
management fad, as, *5-6*
models of, *77-93*
principle of, *10*
school aspiring to become, *3-4*
term as metaphor, *6-9*
Learning school
characteristics of, *24-25*
leading, *140-143*

Machines
organisations as, *6*
Management
learning organisation as fad, *5-6*
managing blocks to
learning, *39-40*
Mandated change
innovation fatigue and, *107-109*
Manifesting leadership, *131-133*
Memory
characteristics of, *64-65*
habits distinguished from, *64-65*
Mental models
sharing, *11-13*
Mentoring, *144-145*
Metaphors
list of, *6-7*
term learning organisation as, *6-9*
using metaphorical thinking, *8-9*
Modelling
characteristics of, *65-66*
Models of learning organisation
characteristics of learning
organisation, *77-85*
energy flow model, *85-93*
generally, *77*
Moral purpose of education, *5-6*
Moving school
characteristics of, *17-18*

stuck school contrasted with, *18*

NVQs
introduction of, *22*
National Curriculum
development of, *22*
effect of, *29*

Organisational learning
balancing and developing
styles, *69-70*
concept of, *4-5, 51-52*
critical awareness, *67-68*
enquiry, *67-68*
experiment, *66-67*
habits, *63-64*
imitation, *65-66*
memory, *64-65*
modelling, *65-66*
style, *58-70*
understanding your
organisation, *52-58*
Organisational politics
attitudes to, *102-104*
Organisational project
opportunity to take lead in, *144*
Organisational toxicity index
(OTI), *96-99*
Organisms
organisations as, *7*

Participative policy making, *78*
Performance orientation
learning orientation and, *30*
Personal development
concept of, *22-23*
Personal mastery
discipline of,*10-11*
Personal perspective on
leadership, *122-124*

Policy making
  participative, *78*
Political systems
  organisations as, *7*
Power
  barriers to change, *110*
  inventory, *137*
  using, *135-137*
Practical barriers to change, *110*
Principle of learning
  organisation, *10*
Psychic prisons
  organisations as, *7*
Psychological barriers to
  change, *110-111*
Pupils
  pupil and teacher learning, *28-29*

Reflecting on learning, *31-32*
Reward flexibility, *79*

School
  aspiring to become learning
    organisation, *3-4*
  assessing stage of consciousness
    of, *15-16*
Search for excellence, *5*
Self-development
  opportunities for all, *81*
Shadow
  demonic or double aspect, *116*
  informal or hidden aspect, *115-116*
  leadership, living with shadow
    side of, *138-139*
  working with, *115-117*
Shared vision
  discipline of, *13*
  inspiring, *129*
Sharing mental models, *11-13*
Skills, abilities and competencies
  concept of, *22*

Stakeholder analysis, *74-75*
Strategy
  learning approach to, *78*
Stuck school
  characteristics of, *17*
  moving school contrasted
    with, *18*
Supporting groups and
  relationships, *45-46*
Systems thinking
  discipline of, *14*

Teachers
  demoralised, *3-4*
  pupil and teacher learning, *28-29*
Team learning
  discipline of, *13-14*
Teams
  learning in, *40-49*
  roles, *43*
  supporting groups and
    relationships, *45-46*
Time
  block to learning, as, *104-106*
  demands, choices and
    constraints, *105-106*
Transactional leadership, *126-127*
Transformational leadership, *127*
Types of learning, *22-24*

Using metaphorical thinking, *8-9*

Value barriers to change, *109*
Valuing difference, *37-38*
Vision
  creating, *134-139*
  inspiring shared vision, *129*
  shared, *13*

Related education management books for schools from Lemos & Crane
Series Editors: Gaynor Smith and Hugh Figgess

Governing Schools through Policy
Jackie Walters and Colin Richardson

"This is an important book. It has the potential to take governors a big step forward towards the role they are intended by law to fulfil." Joan Sallis OBE

Governing Schools through Policy presents a model of school governance that explains how staff and the governing body can concentrate their energies on what they do best within an effective partnership. In clarifying the governor's role, and distinguishing its responsibilities from managerial ones, *Governing Schools through Policy* can enable schools to:

- Relieve governors of time-wasting paper work
- Free them to formulate and then monitor policy
- Establish governors as "leaders' who develop vision
- Manage the relationship between staff, head teacher, governing body and community to raise standards and provide the best possible opportunities for pupils.

Drawn from the authors' nationwide experience, this practical guide is written for school governors, both new and experienced, as well as head teachers, staff and others working in partnership with their governing bodies.

About the authors

Jackie Walters and Colin Richardson have many years' experience of working with school and college governors. Jackie Walters is head of a LEA Governor Support Service and chair of a governing body. Colin Richardson has senior management responsibility for primary and secondary schools in a large city education authority.

ISBN 1-898001-24 Paperback £9.95

Related education management books for schools from Lemos & Crane
Series Editors: Gaynor Smith and Hugh Figgess

Collaborative School Self-Review
Sheila Russell

"This is the right text for those seeking the facts about accountability and school evaluation. It includes planning, monitoring and the preparation, implementation and review of evaluation." Editor's Choice, *Management in Education*

"I commend this book. It has style and significance." Harry Tomlinson, chairman, British Educational Management and Administration Society

The new ideas in *Collaborative School Self-Review* can assist schools to improve and create their own systems for raising standards. In this pioneering book, phrases such as "target setting" and "performance indicators" are made real and useful in practice. Difficult but crucial areas such as classroom observation and evaluation of individual teacher's performance are explored imaginatively.

The author's approach is soundly based in research and highly pragmatic. There is guidance about how schools can evaluate the independent learning of pupils, and the recognition that every school must determine its own unique agenda. A selective monitoring of both maintenance and development activities is shown to be an essential component of the evaluation of quality.

About the author

Sheila Russell, a former teacher and LEA Senior Inspector, is a Visiting Fellow at Leeds Metropolitan University. She has led Ofsted inspections in primary and secondary schools and is the author of *Prepared for Inspection* and *Ready for Action*.

ISBN 1-898001-26-X Paperback £14.95